HISTORY AS SPECTACLE

Charles V, Holy Roman Emperor. Detail of 1531 line engraving by Barthel Beham

HISTORY AS SPECTACLE: CHARLES V AND IMAGERY

Peter Burke
*Emeritus Professor of Cultural History,
Emmanuel College, Cambridge.*

EER
Edward Everett Root, Publishers, Brighton, 2019.

EER

Edward Everett Root, Publishers, Co. Ltd.,
30 New Road, Brighton, Sussex, BN1 1BN, England.
www.eerpublishing.com

edwardeverettroot@yahoo.co.uk
Details of our overseas Agencies are given on our website.

Peter Burke, *History as Spectacle*

First published in Great Britain in 2019.
© Peter Burke 2019.
This edition © Edward Everett Root 2019.

ISBN hardback 978-1-912224-71-5
ISBN paperback 978-1-912224-70-8
ISBN eBook 978-1-911454-73-1

Peter Burke has asserted his right to be identified as the author of this Work in accordance with the Copyright, Designs and Patents Act 1988 as the owner of this Work.

All rights reserved. No part of this publication may be reproduced, stored in a retrieval system or transmitted in any form or by any means, electronic, mechanical, photocopying, recording or otherwise, without the prior permission of the copyright owner.

Cover design by Pageset Limited. Book production by Head & Heart.

Contents

Introduction..vii

History as Spectacle: Charles V and Imagery...........................1

Bibliographical Essay... 139

INTRODUCTION

This new volume consists of a single essay, on the public images of the emperor Charles V (1500-58). It is often said, and correctly, that as our present changes, we look at the past from new perspectives. Today, the different media play an important role in our lives, including our vision of politics. Some politicians have become stars, and in a few countries, from the USA to India, some film stars have become politicians. 'The State as Spectacle' (*L'État-Spectacle*) is the title of a book 'about and against the star system in politics', published in 1977 – and brought up to date in 2009 – by the political scientist Roger-Gérard Schwartzenberg, who is also a member of the Radical Party of the Left and a deputy in the French National Assembly. In similar fashion, the role of advertising in everyday life inspired an earlier book, *The Selling of the President* (1969), an account of the successful campaign of Richard Nixon by the journalist – and novelist – Joe McGinniss.

The concern with the role of the media in politics and the role of politics in the media has inspired historians, and in particular historians of the early modern period, to investigate the representation of political leaders, especially monarchs, in the past. Studies include *Marketing Maximilian* (2008) by the American art historian Larry Silver, on the father of Charles V, and *Selling the Tudor Monarchy* (2009) by the British historian Kevin Sharpe.

The danger of anachronism is an obvious one, and to my mind the titles of those two books, if not their contents, overstep the mark. What is not anachronistic, however, is the idea of politics as spectacle, as theatre, an idea that underlies important historical studies that include Erik Lönnroth on Gustav III of Sweden (1986), entitled 'the great role', and Richard Wortman's study of the Russian monarchy, *Scenarios of Power* (1995-2000). After all, it was Queen Elizabeth I who remarked, in the age of Shakespeare, that 'we princes are set on stages'.

It is indeed for this lack of awareness of the long-playing role of spectacle and performance in political history that I would criticize Schwartzenberg's book, which I read when working on a study of *The Fabrication of Louis XIV* (1992). That study concentrated on the construction of the king's public image and I should confess that it was in part inspired by a report that Saatchi and Saatchi, an advertising agency hired in 1978 to sell Margaret Thatcher, had advised her to take humming lessons in order to lower her voice and so appear more sympathetic to the voting public. From that report it was, dare I say, only a short step to writing about the high heels worn by Louis XIV, a small man, to make himself appear more impressive (more recently, Nicholas Sarkozy, equally small, adopted the same strategy).

It was my book on the 'fabrication' of Louis that led to an invitation from the Belgian historian Hugo Soly to write a similar piece on the fabrication of Charles. The invitation was an attractive

Introduction

one, an encouragement to investigate both the similarities and the differences in the public images of the two monarchs. In both cases, what might be called the 'self-presentation' of the ruler was in fact a collective enterprise involving artists, writers and civil servants. However, this enterprise was relatively decentralized in the earlier example, that of Charles, and relatively centralized in that of Louis, in whose reign a committee was appointed to examine representations of the monarch.

In any case, my commission – a chapter in a huge volume on Charles published on and for the quincentenary of his birth, in the year 2000 – included the posthumous image of the emperor, in academic and popular histories, in historical paintings, in folklore and even on beer-mats. It was fascinating to discover how many and various these images of Charles were, including the national ones, since Charles has been viewed as a Fleming, a Spaniard and a German as well as, like Charlemagne, a good European.

HISTORY AS SPECTACLE:
CHARLES V AND IMAGERY

'*L'histoire de Charles Quint ne peut être que la somme des explications possibles de sa vie, de son oeuvre et de son temps*'. (Fernand Braudel)

It is a historical commonplace that in different periods, people have looked at the past from diverse points of view, reflecting their own preoccupations rather than those of their ancestors, who were contemporaries of the events in question. In an age in which advertising has invaded daily life, and in which political leaders as well as corporations are conscious of the importance of a favourable public 'image', as they often say, it is natural to ask whether this preoccupation had any equivalent in the past. Some historians have asked this question and come up with a positive answer.

Not long after a book about the 'The Selling of the President', dealing with Richard Nixon's election campaign, had been published by an American journalist, Joe McGinniss (1968), a doctoral thesis was submitted to an American university under the title 'The Selling of Louis XII'. 'Selling' may not be the most appropriate metaphor for a sixteenth-century monarch, at a time when the style of rulers was rarely if ever demotic (Gustav Vasa of Sweden, who sometimes addressed his people in the market-place of a small town, is one of the few examples to come readily to mind). However, following the lead of recent studies of the emperor Rudolf II, for example, of King Francis I, and of Louis XIV, one might reasonably speak of 'propaganda' for Charles V, of the 'imagined' Charles, or of the 'fabrication' of the emperor.

The essential point to make at the start is that the images, whether literary or visual, should not be studied and will not be studied here as unproblematic 'reflections' of the reality of the time. They always represent viewpoints and on occasion they were subject to conscious manipulation. The main reason for devoting so much attention to these images is not that they were reflections of something else but that they were events themselves, 'media events' of course, but events with consequences, affecting contemporary perceptions of the emperor and so helping to shape reactions to his actions and policies. In other words, all history involves representation, and all representations are part of history.

Impression management

The apparent analogy between the sixteenth and the twentieth centuries must not be pushed further than it will reasonably go. Charles V could not turn to an advertising agency such as Saatchi and Saatchi for advice on improving his image, as Mrs Thatcher did in the 1980s. All the same, the basic idea of 'self-presentation' or 'impression management' was not invented by an agency.

It was not even devised by the American sociologist Erving Goffman, whose discussion of the topic in *The Presentation of Self in Everyday Life* (1959) rapidly became a classic and underlies many later treatments of the theme. On the contrary, in the sixteenth century the idea was already a familiar one.

For example, the importance of 'giving a good impression' is discussed at length in one of the most famous of Renaissance dialogues, 'The Courtier' (*Il Cortegiano*) first published in 1528 and written by Baldassare Castiglione (1478-1529), the papal nuncio to Charles V and a man once described by the emperor as 'one of the finest gentlemen in the world (*uno de los mejores caballeros del mundo*)'. In this dialogue, the leading characters explain in detail the appropriate manner in which the ideal courtier should walk, gesture, dance, or speak in public, always with an eye on the audience. The author was superlatively self-conscious in this respect, but so were some of his sixteenth-century readers, to judge from the care with which they underlined and annotated key passages of the text.

In the case of Charles V, however, what we see – intermittently, wherever the surviving evidence allows – is considerably more than self-conscious behaviour in the manner recommended in *The Courtier*. We see the conscious pursuit of glory, of honour, and of reputation, or what one of the imperial secretaries, Francisco de los Cobos, described to Charles as 'the great name of a great king' (*el gran nombre de rey grande*), while an imperial ambassador, cardinal Juan Pardo de Tavera (1472-1545) referred to 'your imperial reputation' (*su imperial reputación*). Phrases such as 'to gain and increase honour and reputation' (*gagner et accroistre honneur et réputation*) recur in official documents. That Charles personally took this point to heart is revealed by the language of the political testaments which he composed for the benefit of his son Prince Philip, recommending various ways in which the young prince could gain 'honour and reputation'.

Later historians such as William Robertson (below) went further in this direction, accusing Charles of both simulation and dissimulation, while the nineteenth-century Belgian historian Alexandre Henne went further still and described the emperor as an accomplished actor whose piety, mildness, clemency, and even sincerity were so many performances (*il jouait la piété, comme il jouait souvent la sincérité, la douceur, la clémence*).

In the case of the emperor's role in certain public rituals, at least, the appropriate term would seem to be not mere self-consciousness but 'stage-management'. For an example of the careful organisation of an event in which Charles played the central part, one might take the annual Maundy Thursday ritual of washing the feet of the poor, a theatre of humility in which the emperor re-enacted the role of Christ washing the feet of his disciples, as described in the New Testament. In 1544 this drama was staged in the German city of Speyer. It is worth noting that the poor were carefully selected for the occasion. Bartholomaeus Sastrow (1520-1603), later burgomaster of Stralsund, who happened to be in Speyer at the time, noted in his journal that 'Care had been taken to ascertain that those people were in good health, nay their feet had been washed beforehand'.

Sastrow's story is confirmed by a similar account of the emperor's visit to Mantua at the same time of year in 1530. On this occasion, Charles asked for thirteen poor who were `clean and healthy (*nette et senza male alcuno*)'. They were asked to wash their own feet and they were then taken to the monastery of St Agnes. On their arrival, their feet were washed again, first by an imperial chaplain and then by a bishop, before the emperor arrived to perform the ritual.

As these examples suggest, by the early sixteenth century the public image of rulers was considered too important to leave to the individuals concerned. As Queen Elizabeth I of England once observed, 'We princes ... are set on stages', observed by all the world. Communication was an art, indeed by this time it had become a profession, that of the rhetorician. For this reason it is only realistic, however paradoxical this may seem, to view the 'self-presentation' of sixteenth-century monarchs as a collective enterprise of fabrication.

In the case of Charles, the enterprise was a truly international one in which hundreds of individuals played their part: poets, painters, printers, official historians, weavers (notably Willem Pannemaker, a tapestry-weaver from Brussels), armourers (notably Desiderius Colman, a goldsmith from Augsburg), and an elaborate hierarchy of clerks and secretaries. Not only the emperor's letters but his speeches too were generally composed for him by his counsellors.

A few individuals may be regarded not so much as assistants as managers of the imperial image. These individuals included the grand chancellors Guillaume de Croy, seigneur de Chièvres (1458-1521) and his successor Mercurio Arborio de Gattinara (1465-1530); Charles's aunt, Margaret of Austria (1480-1530), the Regent of the Netherlands till her death in 1530, and a major patron of the arts; and Nicholas Perrenot de Granvelle (1486-1550) who spent a lifetime in imperial service. When this army of image-makers, managers and assistants is taken into account, Charles may appear not as a historical force so much as a space in which other people acted in his name. All the same, as he slowly developed from an adolescent prince into an experienced middle-aged ruler, the emperor gradually took more initiatives in this domain as he did in others. Charles's increasing personal interest in his image will be discussed in more detail later in this chapter.

In the analysis of the process of self-presentation, it is important to avoid two opposite dangers. On one side there is the risk of literal-mindedness, of taking at face value what was intended as a figure of speech, whether metaphor or hyperbole. On the other side there is the danger of what might be called historiographical paranoia, in other words of seeing manipulation and conspiracy everywhere. It is worth emphasising that whatever his personal virtues or defects, which did not go unnoticed at the time, the emperor was also regarded as the embodiment of certain values.

In any case, the imperial image was not a construction out of nothing. It is more illuminating to view it as the result of a collective enterprise of *bricolage*, making use of fragments from earlier traditions, both classical and medieval, but combining them in new ways whenever that appeared to be politically useful. However, too much emphasis should not be placed on instrumental notions such as 'uses' or 'functions'. Like Charles's other subjects, the fabricators themselves saw the emperor through the filter of tradition. Like other rulers, but to a greater degree than most of them, Charles had inherited charisma.

The media

Although the term 'media' – literally the 'means' of communication – now evokes the world of newspapers, radio and television, the term is still worth using here because it helps us to think of the different forms of communication available in a particular place and time as a kind of package, working on the public not in isolation but in interaction with one another.

Painting and sculpture, for example, were employed to represent the major events of the reign, especially successful battles, as well as to portray the emperor himself. Easier for us to forget, although quite obvious to contemporaries with a knowledge of heraldry (an indispensable part of the education of noblemen at this time), were the many indirect representations of the emperor by means of his personal device or his coat of arms, each of its many compartments or 'quarterings' referring to one of the states he ruled or claimed – castles for Castille (a typical heraldic pun), lions for León, pomegranates for Granada, vertical stripes (in heraldic language 'pales') for Aragon, chains for Navarre, a cross for Jerusalem, and so on. The imperial shield was often supported on the breast of a crowned double-headed black eagle, the symbol of the Habsburg dynasty, and it was usually surrounded by the collar of the Order of the Golden Fleece, with alternating flints and steels with the fleece itself as a pendant.

Portraits were particularly important in the creation of Charles's public image, and by 1525 or thereabouts, the workshop of Bernard van Orley (c. 1492-1542) in Brussels was already producing multiple copies of the emperor's likeness. The full-length life-size portraits now known to art historians as 'state portraits' were a new genre at this time, considered especially appropriate for the representation of important people, and several of Charles's artists knew well how to exploit it, beginning with Jacob Seisenegger (1505-67), whose full-length portrait of the emperor with his dog (1532) was considered so successful that Titian was asked to copy it. Titian went on to produce the two most impressive portraits of the emperor, both in the year 1548. One is the seated figure now in Munich, 'the first self-sufficient unallegorical and unceremonial single portrait' at full length, as the art historian Erwin Panofsky has described it, showing a Charles who is 'withdrawn, watchful and ineffably lonely'. The other is the still more famous equestrian portrait, to be discussed below.

The painted image of the emperor might also be seen in glass, in the stained glass in the north transept of Brussels cathedral, for example, designed by Orley and showing Charles and his wife on their knees, accompanied by Charlemagne. To a select audience, illuminated manuscripts presented a vivid image of the emperor's deeds, as in the case of the manuscript of the Bruges entry of 1515, which belonged to Charles' sister Maria of Hungary (1505-58); or the manuscript of the prophecy of Daniel, illuminated by Jörg Breu the younger and now in the Escorial; or the epic poem by Euralio d'Ascoli, *L'impresa del aquila*, illustrated by the Croat painter Giulio Clovio (1498-1578) and presented to Charles in 1543; or the manuscript history of the emperor's deeds by Erard de la Mark, now in the Royal Library in Brussels; or finally the image of Charles as head of the prestigious military Order of the Golden Fleece, painted by the Netherlander Simon Bening (c. 1483-1561) for the register of the order.

Tapestry, sometimes described by contemporaries as 'woven painting', was another prestigious genre at this time, designed by leading court artists such as Orley and Jan Corneliszoon Vermeyen (c. 1500-59), and considered as especially suitable for the representation of elaborate scenes such as battles. This medium was also specially appropriate for an itinerant ruler such as Charles, since his favourite pieces could accompany him wherever he went and thus frame his public appearances, his coronation and abdication, for instance, ase we shall see later in this chapter. The importance of tapestry was also that it was a form of mechanical reproduction, allowing the same image to be seen in various places at the same time.

Statues of the emperor in different materials included the wooden bust of the seventeen-year old prince by Conrad Meit (c. 1506-1551); the stone relief of the emperor on horseback by Hans Daucher (c. 1485-1538), and the unusual image of Charles in metal (wearing armour which can be removed) suppressing Fury, the work of Leone Leoni (c. 1509-90). These statues were designed to be seen indoors, since the erection of permanent statues of rulers on public squares was not yet a general custom. The emperor, like other rulers of his time, had to be satisfied with the building of arches and gates in his honour, like the Keizerspoort at Antwerp, erected in 1545, or by temporary monuments, like the equestrian statue of the emperor commissioned by the signoria of Siena from Domenico Beccafumi for Charles's entry into the city in 1536, or the statue displayed at the wedding of Cosimo de' Medici in Florence in 1539.

The emperor's image might also be seen in miniature form on jewels and on cameos. Mechanically-reproduced images of the emperor included official seals, stamps for bindings, and of course the coins and medals issued during his reign. The golden and silver *carolus* and the silver *teston* were probably the means by which Charles's more wealthy subjects became most familiar with the features of the emperor.

A relatively new genre of representation, invented in fifteenth-century Italy on the model of classical coins, was the bronze medal. Rulers or their advisers quickly realised the potential of the new medium for disseminating favourable images of themselves and their policies. Charles's medals often combined the portrait of the emperor on one side (the 'obverse') with representations of major events of the reign, such as the victories of Tunis and Mühlberg, on the other (the 'reverse'), with appropriate inscriptions in order to guide the viewers' interpretation of the images. The language of these inscriptions was usually Latin, partly in homage to classical antiquity and partly to ensure the international circulation of the medals, at least among male elites. The rise of the German Renaissance medal in the early sixteenth century, like the rise of the state portrait, happened to coincide with the adulthood of Charles and the new genre was quickly exploited by artists working for the emperor or his subjects, by Friedrich Hagenauer (c. 1500-c. 1546), of Strasbourg and Hans Reinhart (d. 1581) of Leipzig, for example, or Hans Schwarz (c. 1492-) and Christoph Weiditz (c. 1500-1559), both of Augsburg. Some twenty German medals representing Charles have survived.

Architecture too could carry a political message. Charles was a great traveller who usually occupied temporary accommodation and so he was not such a great builder as some of his contemporaries, notably Francis I. All the same, one architectural project at least seems to have been planned as a statement of his position. The circular palace at Granada begun in the 1520s and designed by Pedro Machuca (d. 1550), a Spaniard who had just returned from Rome, was built in a pure classical style, probably in order to evoke the atmosphere of imperial Rome and to make a dramatic contrast with the traditional Islamic architecture of the neighbouring Alhambra. The inscription on the palace made the glorification of the emperor explicit and ran as follows: ALWAYS AUGUST, PIOUS, SUCCESSFUL, UNCONQUERED (*SEMPER AUGUSTUS PIUS FELIX INVICTISSIMUS*).

Speeches, whether made by the emperor himself or by a representative, were also important in spreading information about imperial policies, or at least about what the ruling circles wanted people to believe were the imperial policies. The first such speech, to the States-General in Brussels, goes back to 1507, when Charles was only seven, and shows that chancellor Chièvres was already training the prince to appear on the public stage. Another, delivered before leaving Spain, was printed in Augsburg in 1518 under the title *Adlocutio*. A better-known example is that of the speech at the Cortes of Santiago in 1520, given in the emperor's name and indeed in his presence by Pedro Mota, bishop of Badajoz and one of his most important advisers at this time. Yet another well-known example is the imperial speech to the Cortes of Valladolid in 1523, which begins with the words 'I love these kingdoms of mine so much (*Yo amo y quiero tanto estos mis Reynos*)'. Even more celebrated at the time was Charles's speech to the pope in 1536, delivered in person, in Spanish, and lasting one and a half hours (not so long by the standards of the speeches and sermons of the time). Versions of this speech were soon available in print in Latin, French, Flemish and German. Most famous of all was Charles's abdication speech, which the ailing emperor delivered in Brussels to a weeping audience.

Official letters were another means for the presentation of the public image of heads of state. Hence the importance of the institution of the chancery in the later Middle Ages and the Renaissance, when humanists skilled in rhetoric and in writing a fluent Latin in the style of Cicero were in demand in both republics and courts. Famous examples include Leonardo Bruni in early fifteenth-century Florence and Pietro Bembo and Jacopo Sadoleto in the Rome of Pope Leo X. Laws had a similar function of representation, notably the new law-code for the empire (promulgated in 1532), which was known in honour of Charles as the 'Carolina'.

Even treaties may be regarded as a means of self-presentation for the emperor. For example, the texts of the treaties of Madrid, Barcelona, Bologna, and Nice all included preambles explaining the reasons for the negotiations. Thus the treaty of Madrid (1526) explained the need for the 'Christian commonwealth *(la république chrétienne)*' to unite in order to make possible common action against the 'tyranny of the unbelieving Turks *(la tyrannie des mécréants turcs)*' and the 'extirpation of the errors of the Lutheran sect *(l'extirpation des erreurs de la secte lutherienne)*'. In similar fashion, the treaty of Barcelona (1529) declared that despite the 'most happy victory' of the imperial army at Naples, Charles was not elated by his success. On the contrary, he was all the more willing to make peace *(Non quidem ea victoria elatus Caesar, sed tanto magis ad pacem propensus)*. These treaties were 'published' at the time in the sense of being solemnly read aloud in public, as in the case of the treaty of Madrid, which was immediately proclaimed in the cities of Antwerp, Rome and Florence.

The relatively new medium of print also made a major contribution to the diffusion of Charles's image. Regular newspapers did not come into existence until the early seventeenth century, but all the major events of Charles's reign were described in occasional news-sheets, whether official or unofficial, whether in German, Spanish, Flemish, or Italian. As for other texts, images of the emperor were spread via a considerable variety of genres such as epics, odes, letters, histories and even prophecies. The references to Charles in the famous epic by Ludovico Ariosto (1474-1533), *Orlando Furioso*, reached a particularly wide audience, since this book was one of the best-sellers of the day.

Print was used to reproduce images as well as texts. The importance of these printed images, woodcuts, engravings and occasionally etchings, should become clear by examining the illustrations to this chapter. These printed images, woodcuts, engravings and occasionally etchings, were both common and, in all probability, extremely influential. Stories could be told by printing a series of images, like the sixteen woodcuts, published in Venice in 1530, which presented the emperor's entry into Bologna in 1529. To look at them in sequence, like the more famous series of images of the coronation cavalcade, by Robert Péril and Nicholas Hogenberg (c. 1500-1539), gives an impression not unlike that of watching a film about Charles.

Printed texts also did much to spread favourable images of the emperor. Treaties, for instance, were often published as well as proclaimed. The peace of 1526 and the truce of 1537, for example, were printed by the Roman printer Antonio Blado. Pamphlets were sometimes printed with official encouragement. In the Southern Netherlands alone, for example, at least 63 pamphlets in Dutch and twelve more in French were sponsored by the government between 1520 and 1555. Printed versions of some of the emperor's speeches were in circulation at the time, for instance the 'Speech to the Spanish Lords (*Oratione alli signori spagnoli*), published in Italian in 1526 by another Roman printer, Francesco Minizio Calvo.

Erasmus and Charles's court preacher fray Antonio de Guevara (c. 1481-1545) both addressed treatises of advice to the young emperor. However, the books were not only presented to Charles, they were also published. The act of publication shows that these two humanists were also engaged in the enterprise of presenting the emperor to others. Erasmus's *Institutio principis Christiani* ('The Education of a Christian Prince') was published in Basel in 1516 – in contrast to Machiavelli's *Prince*, which took the form of private advice to the Medici family and was published only after the author's death. Guevara's – largely fictional – biography of the emperor Marcus Aurelius, first published in Valladolid in 1528 and often reprinted, advised Charles to take Marcus as a guide, master, friend, example and rival. That Charles did see himself reflected in this mirror of princes is suggested by the fact that he gave prince Philip advice in his political `testaments' of 1543 and 1548 in much the same manner that Guevara's Marcus was represented as giving counsel to his son.

The imperial image may also be said to have been constructed out of people, who were walking 'representations' as well as 'representatives' of the emperor. For example, Charles's queen, Isabel of Portugal, 'La Serenisima Emperatriz Reina', as she was described at the time, took his place in 1532 when he was unavoidably absent from Spain. The Viceroys of Aragon, Catalonia, Valencia, Sardinia, Naples, Sicily, New Spain, and Peru were, as their name implies, deputy kings who took Charles's place in ritual events such as state entries into cities as well as making administrative decisions on the emperor's behalf. Pedro Alvarez de Toledo, viceroy of Naples, Ferrante Gonzaga, viceroy of Sicily and their colleagues gave Charles's subjects lasting impressions of the emperor's regime. In similar fashion the regents of the Netherlands, Charles's aunt Margaret of Austria and his sister Maria of Hungary, represented the emperor. At assemblies such as the Reichstag or the Cortes, Charles was sometimes present by proxy through an official spokesman or *Stellvertreter*. Ambassadors too should be regarded not only as negotiators or information gatherers but as images of and spokesmen for the emperor. All these people may be described as agents of self-presentation at a distance.

Public rituals or festivals may be viewed as multi-media representations of the emperor. The imperial election at Frankfurt, for instance, Charles's two coronations at Aachen (Aix-la-Chapelle) and Bologna, and the coronation of Charles's brother Ferdinand as King of the Romans may all be interpreted in this way. So may religious rituals like that of Maundy Thursday, described above. So may feudal rituals. When Gattinara was made imperial chancellor at Zaragoza in 1518, for instance, he took an oath, knelt, and placed his hands between those of Charles in the traditional medieval gesture of fidelity, making clear to the onlooker his dependence on his master (although in practice the chancellor often told the young emperor what to do).

The representative assemblies of Charles's realms – the German 'Diet' or *Reichstag*, the Spanish *Cortes* and the States-General of the Netherlands – may be seen as so many stages on which the emperor presented himself. For example, at the first session of the *Cortes* of Santiago in 1520, Charles was 'seated in his royal chair', while the deputies told him in traditional Spanish style that they kissed his hands and feet. At the ceremonial opening of the *Reichstag* at Worms in 1521, for instance, or at Speyer in 1526, there was a procession to the cathedral followed by Mass and a procession to the Rathaus. The closing of the assembly or 'recess' (*Abschied*) was also ritualized.

Although they took place before an extremely select audience, the rituals of the regular chapters of the Order of the Golden Fleece should not be forgotten. Founded in 1429 by Philip the Good Duke of Burgundy in order to encourage a crusade, and organised around a symbol which had both classical and christian resonance (the fleece was associated with Gideon as well as Jason), this order of chivalry was taken over by the Emperor Maximilian after his marriage with Maria of Burgundy. The significance of the Golden Fleece for Charles, who was Grand Master of the order, is associated with his concern for his Burgundian inheritance and also with his self-image as a crusader. Its importance for him is revealed not only in his portraits, in which he is generally represented wearing the collar of the order, but also in the special ceremony before the emperor's abdication, in which he resigned his Grand Mastership.

Charles began his reign by touring the provinces he had inherited, and in a sense he never stopped doing this. He was always on the road, as his numerous state entries into cities (from the declaration of his majority in 1515 onwards) remind us. The solemn 'entry' (*entrata, entrée, Einreitung*), may be seen as the performance of a drama, or more exactly, of two simultaneous dramas. In one sense, the emperor was the main actor, the central figure of grand processions or parades with infantry, cavalry, artillery (in Bologna, Rome and elsewhere), winding through the streets of the city, while the audience were the townspeople to whom money was thrown and who reciprocated with shouts of 'Cesare Cesare, Carlo Carlo, Imperio Imperio' and so on.

In another sense, the ruler and his entourage were the audience, spectators of one scene after another organized by the municipal authorities. The drama might begin outside the city, as it did at Aachen in 1520 or at Augsburg in 1530, when the electors, followed by eight citizens, followed by the papal legate, all met Charles in the countryside in order to escort him to the city itself. It would usually include triumphal arches, speeches, and symbolic gifts to the emperor, such as the keys of the city, a horse or (in Paris in 1540), a lifesize silver statue of Hercules.

From the artistic point of view, the most important of these entries were the Italian ones, from Bologna in 1530 to Milan in 1541. From the political point of view, however, all these events were important in an age when the state was personalised and subjects wanted to see in the flesh the ruler they had been taught to regard as a father. Indeed, it has been suggested that if Philip II had spent more time in the Netherlands, or Philip IV in Catalonia, the rebellion of these regions might have been avoided.

The script of these imperial dramas were often published at the time, allowing a second and much larger audience to participate vicariously in the events, while the original spectators could learn the precise meaning of the shows they had recently witnessed. Francesco Calvo published the Seville entry of 1526, for example, while Antonio Blado published the Messina, Florence and Rome entries of 1535-6. The publication of the text sometimes took place very soon after the event. A letter describing the coronation at Aachen on 23 October 1520 was published in the city on the 25th, while an Italian version of the account was printed, according to its colophon, on the

24th. The texts were often illustrated, and independent printed images of these events were also in circulation.

How many hours of the emperor's day were taken up by ritual activities is difficult to say. The problem is that it is difficult, if not impossible, to decide what actions count as ritual in the case of an individual whose daily life – dressing, eating, and so on – was ritualized to a considerable degree. For example, until he was fifty Charles regularly took some of his meals in public, abandoning the habit around 1550 either because he was losing his teeth, as one nineteenth-century historian suggested, or because he was increasingly attracted by the Spanish ideal of the hidden ruler. In practice, the emperor can have had little 'private' life, although he is known to have taken mistresses after the death of his wife (notably Margaret Gheest, the mother of Margareta of Parma, and Barbara Blomberg, the mother of Don Juan of Austria). Government sources naturally made no reference to such activities, which from the official point of view were invisible. Only foreign sources reveal Charles's interest in sex. Among these, the reports by the Venetian ambassadors stand out for both their detachment and their concrete details. The Venetians did not need to flatter the emperor when they wrote home and may, as republicans, have been less sensitive to the imperial charisma. In any case they sometimes describe the emperor when he was more or less off-duty, relaxing by playing chess with his courtiers.

Travel was another example of the ritualization of the everyday and another means of self-presentation. Indeed, in Charles's case it may be viewed as one of the most effective means employed in order to 'broadcast' news of imperial policies. It was also a way to fill the gap between the vast size of the empire and the need of the emperor's subjects both to see and to be seen by him. Charles's abdication speech notes that in the course of four decades as emperor he had made forty journeys; ten visits to the Low Countries, nine to Germany, seven to Italy, six to Spain, four to France, two to England and two to North Africa. The interest in precise figures, including his seventeen attacks of gout, reappears in Charles's memoirs and his political testaments and seems to have been one of the personal characteristics of the emperor.

The relatively rare meetings between rulers were also ritualized. They generally required careful planning and the tactful management (on the part of professionals such as the imperial majordomo Pedro de la Cueva), of competing and irreconcilable claims to be at the centre of the stage. In May 1538, for example, at Nice, the emperor and the King of France both met pope Paul IV but they did not encounter each other there (a meeting was eventually organised at Aigues-Mortes). Meeting the pope posed less of a problem than meeting another king because there was a traditional ritual script available for such occasions. In 1530, for example, Charles knelt and kissed pope Clement VII's foot outside the church of San Petronio in Bologna. In 1536, it was Paul IV's foot that he kissed at the portico of St Peter's in Rome.

Charles himself should also be regarded as an image. Indeed, he was once described, in 1517, by the English diplomat Christopher Tunstall as 'as immoveable as an idol' (a posture which was, or was becoming at this time, a Spanish royal tradition). Charles represented himself in the sense of playing the role of emperor in public, listening to supplicants, taking their petitions and so on. Contemporaries, whether or not they were interested in the science of physiognomy, paid considerable attention to Charles's appearance. For instance, his drooping jaw (a Habsburg characteristic), was sometimes the object of unfavourable comments. On the other hand, according to the Italian historian Paolo Giovio (c. 1483-1552), in the vivid pen-portrait of the emperor which he inserted into the twenty-seventh book of his famous *History of his Own Time*, the emperor's prominent nose was a sign of his clemency or magnanimity, and he noted that it would have been interpreted in this way by the ancient Persians. Charles's high forehead (*la fronte spatiosa*) and pale blue eyes (*gli occhi cesii*) were interpreted by one Venetian ambassador, Federico Badoer, as signs of the great intellectual vigour of the emperor.

Charles's authority was fabricated in part by means of his clothes, his armour, and even the cut of his hair and beard. The Lombard humanist Pietro Martire d'Anghiera, in a letter of 1521, reported a rumour that Charles was already bearded (*aiunt ... barbatum iam esse*), which is not implausible, since his contemporary Henry VIII had recently grown a beard. The age of clean-shaven monarchs such as Maximilian and Louis XII of France was over. Charles is also shown as bearded on a relief of 1522 by Hans Daucher. His beard was probably adopted as a sign of virility, or as Giovio suggested, of gravity. According to a contemporary panegyrist, Guillaume Snouckaert, Charles's beard – square in Germany, pointed in Italy, and so on – revealed the emperor's ability to adapt himself to the customs of his different dominions. Whether or not this was a matter of policy, the portraits of Charles confirm the suggestion that in the course of the reign the imperial beard was trimmed in a number of different styles, now shorter, now longer.

Equally significant was the change from long hair (in the manner of his grandfather Maximilian, for example, or Louis XII), to short hair in the manner of Francis I and Henry VIII, or indeed – according to the Spanish historian Alfonso de Ulloa – of the Roman emperors. The change is generally is said to have been made in 1529, shortly before the expedition to Italy, though the wedding portrait of Charles by Jean Mone (d. c. 1549) suggests that the change had already taken place by 1526. The courtiers, as courtiers will, rapidly followed their master's example.

On the other hand, at least one printer was slow to respond to this change in Charles's appearance, and the woodcut on the title-page of the description of the Augsburg Reichstag of 1530 represents an adolescent emperor with long hair, presumably using a woodcut which was already in stock rather than making a new one for the occasion. That Charles was personally concerned with these details of his appearance is suggested by the fact that when he found his first white hairs, in Naples, in 1535 – as he once confessed to the French admiral Gaspar de Coligny – he was careful to have these signs of age removed.

Clothes too helped create the image of the emperor, notably the costume he wore for special occasions like the coronation at Aachen, when Charles was dressed in blue for his entry into the city and gold, silver and crimson for the coronation itself. On the latter occasion, his hat was surmounted by white feathers and he rode a white horse. Armour was a symbol of courage and power as well as a means of protection in battle, and Charles wore it on some state occasions, such as his entry into Bologna in 1530. He even owned a suit of armour in the ancient Roman style, made in Italy and given to him by the duke of Urbino.

Dignity was added to the emperor's appearance by the gold collar of the Order of the Golden Fleece, which he seems to have worn on all important occasions.

On the other hand, the simplicity of Charles's costume was often the object of comment, usually unfavourable comment, as in the case of his clothes of violet velvet for the Roman entry of 1536. For the Genoa entry of 1529, the emperor wore white, while for the Paris entry of 1540, according to his official chronicler Alonso de Santa Cruz (book 4, section 55), he 'dressed in a black Italian cloak and a coat of black cloth and a cap of black cloth, to the great surprise of the French, who thought that His Majesty ought to have dressed in the style appropriate to his rank and fame (*vestido de un capote italiano negro y sayo de paño negro y una gorra de paño negro, lo cual era grande admiración de los franceses, que pensaban que había de venir vestido Su Majestad conforme al nombre y estado que tenía*)'.

Turning to everyday clothes, the Venetian ambassador Nicolò Tiepolo recorded his surprise at the emperor's lack of magnificence, describing him as `rather simple in his clothing (*nel vestir suo ... parca assai*)'. Tiepolo's colleagues Bernardo Navagero and Marino Cavalli also noted that Charles was more modest than imperial in his dress, that `he does not dress ... with pomp (*non veste ... pomposamente*)'. Perhaps this choice was itself a form of distinction, a way of standing out from a glittering court, like the black which would be favoured by his son Philip II. However, it should be added that Tiepolo did not find the imperial court glittering at all, but on the contrary, somewhat shabby. The English humanist Roger Ascham made a similar comment on the emperor's clothes when he visited Charles at Augsburg in 1551 and found him wearing a simple 'gown of black taffeta' and 'a furred nightcap'. The emperor was not feeling well on this occasion, but the fact that he allowed himself to be seen in informal clothes at all is a reminder that he was not equally concerned with all aspects of his self-presentation. Titian found a way to dignify this simplicity in his famous portrait of the seated emperor of 1548 in which the traditional throne and sceptre are replaced by armchair and stick, and Charles's costume lacks signs of rank apart from a discreetly displayed pendant of a golden fleece.

In the case of Charles's posture, gestures, and language – as in that of his off-duty activities – the cool regard of outsiders such as the Venetian ambassadors once again makes a valuable antidote to flattering accounts from inside the system. Their references to his drooping jaw remind us that all the emperor's portraits, however strong their 'reality effect', edited out this defect and so produced an idealised image. Again, according to a Venetian report of 1521, Charles spoke with some difficulty. Another Venetian ambassador, Gasparo Contarini, in 1525, was even more frank: 'In speaking he sometimes stammers, especially at the end of the sentence *(nel parlare, massime nel finire della clausula, balbutisce qualche parola)*'. Federico Badoer confirmed this impression in a report of 1557, in which he explains that the almost toothless emperor tended to swallow his words so that they were scarcely intelligible *(non può congiungere li denti e nel finire le parole no è ben inteso)*. On the other hand, it was generally admitted that Charles was a good horseman, no small advantage in an age which viewed the relation between a ruler and his subjects as much the same as that between a rider and his horse.

The emperor's lack of expressiveness, which led an English diplomat, as we have seen, to compare him to an idol, was also noted more than once by the Venetian ambassadors. 'Not very affable (*molto poco affabile*)', 'Does not seem to be affable (*Non pare ... affabile*)' are among the comments. Other observers made a similar point in a more charitable way. Paolo Giovio, for instance, praised Charles's apparent freedom from emotions such as anger (*irarum impetus*), and his possession of the royal quality of 'gravity'. One of the Venetians concurred. 'Grave in manner, but not cruel or severe (*L'aspetto grave, non però crudele ne severo*)' was his verdict. In the sixteenth century, gravity was a quality associated with Spaniards in particular. It looks as if Charles was acquiring a Spanish style in the mid-1520s, or at the very least as if he was already perceived by foreigners in this way.

The emperor's image, like that of other important people of the time, was enhanced by a number of accessories or 'properties' in the theatrical sense of the term. In the first place, the imperial insignia, the crown, the sceptre, the orb, and the sword of state (a new sword was designed for the emperor by the famous goldsmith Wenzel Jamnitzer). These objects were only used on special occasions such as coronations and even then they were generally carried by great nobles, in procession for example. All the same, these insignia were inseparable from representations of the emperor.

The imperial insignia were supplemented by other accessories. The *baldachino* under which he rode at Bologna in 1530 assimilated the emperor to the pope and also to Christ, since the Blessed Sacrament was displayed in this way at the feast of Corpus Christi. Other impressive properties included Charles's horses, for example the white horses he mounted for his coronations at Aachen and Bologna, the horse he was given for his entry into Messina 1535, and so on. In representations of the emperor by artists, if not in real life, he sometimes wore a laurel crown, carried a baton, and was surrounded by trophies, eagles, prisoners, and personified virtues, victories, rivers, cities, and so on, like Augustus before him and other rulers, notably Louis XIV, in later centuries. Even in less formal portraits Charles is almost invariably shown wearing the collar of the Order of the Golden Fleece, an image which functioned as a reminder to viewers of both the chivalric identity of the emperor and his Burgundian roots (since it was at the court of Burgundy that the order was founded). His coat-of-arms was also an integral part of Charles's image, and one to which contemporary noble observers, at least, would have been trained to give close attention.

Imperial traditions

Whether they are to be regarded as constraints or resources, or both, the traditions concerning the presentation of monarchs obviously need to be taken into account if we are to understand either the forms which were taken by Charles's public image or the interest which he showed in it. Among these, pride of place should be given to the Habsburg traditions which Charles may be said to have `inherited' from his grandfather Maximilian along with his dominions. The emperor Maximilian (1459-1519) was a man concerned to an almost obsessional degree with his self-image and with the way in which he would be remembered by posterity.

This concern was made vividly apparent not only by the

portraits which he commissioned, but also by his patronage of scholars such as the Austrian humanist Johannes Stabius (d. 1522), and above all by his grandiose tomb in the Hofkirche in Innsbruck, planned to include forty statues of Maximilian's ancestors and thirty-four busts of Roman emperors, besides a number of saints. Some of the artists working for Charles, the Netherlander Bernard van Orley and the Germans Jörg Breu the elder (c. 1475-1537) and Hans Schäufelein (c. 1480-c. 1540), for example, had previously been in the service of Maximilian. Indeed, Schäufelein's woodcut of the triumphal procession of Charles echoes an earlier image of his representing Maximilian.

Maximilian's 'self-stylization' (*Selbststilisierung*), as one scholar, H. O. Burger, has called it, is clear enough in the *Historia Friderici et Maximiliani*, an autobiography which he dictated to his secretary for presentation to his grandson, who would dictate his own memoirs some sixty years later. The process of self-presentation is even more transparent in the semi-autobiographical romances along the lines of the stories of King Arthur which the emperor composed with the assistance of his secretaries, *Theuerdank* in verse and *Weisskunig* in prose. It is these texts which have given Maximilian his posthumous reputation as 'the last knight' (*Der letzte Ritter*), the incarnation of late medieval chivalry. A presentation copy of the manuscript of *Weisskunig*, made for Charles in his grandfather's lifetime, is still to be seen in Vienna. As for *Theuerdank*, it was published in a sumptuous illustrated folio volume in Nuremberg in 1517.

Charles V's other grandfather was Charles the Bold, Duke of Burgundy, and the importance of Burgundian traditions at the imperial court has often been noted. Charles was born in Ghent, and the men in charge of his education were Netherlanders, the

Seigneur de Chièvres and Adrian of Utrecht, later pope. The Order of the Golden Fleece was a Burgundian order of chivalry. The elaborate court ritual which Charles introduced to Spain in the late 1540s was essentially a Burgundian ritual.

Also of great importance for the image of Charles was what might be called the imperial millenarian tradition. The idea of a succession of four world empires, of which the last was the Roman, had been put forward by Paulus Orosius, a younger contemporary of Augustine, early in the fifth century, in his *History against the Pagans*. Some Christians had long been expecting the coming of the so-called 'Last World Emperor', who might reign for a century or more and in whose time the Jews and the pagans would be converted. His reign would be followed by the 'millennium', the thousand-year reign of Christ in this world, and that in turn would be followed by the Last Judgement. At the time of the Crusades, the hope of the conversion of the Muslims was incorporated into this tradition.

The expected imminent conversion of the world was often described in the imagery of 'one flock' under 'one shepherd', as it was, for example, in the writings of the fourteenth-century French Franciscan Jean de Roquetaillade. The term 'shepherd' was an allusion to the famous passage in the Gospel of St John (10, 16), in which Jesus says 'I am the good shepherd: I know my own and my own know me ... And I have other sheep, that are not of this fold; I must bring them also, and they will heed my voice. So there shall be one flock, one shepherd'.

The pope, of course, considered himself the shepherd of all Christians or *pastor universalis*. However, in the long Italian conflict between 'Guelfs' (the partisans of the pope) and 'Ghibellines' (the supporters of the emperor), the latter attributed to their leader a religious as well as a worldly role. It was widely believed that the Church would pass through a period of tribulation and reform, in which the emperor would play an important part. From the mid-fourteenth century onwards, the time of the 'Great Schism' and the scandal of rival popes excommunicating each other, many people expected the coming of a ruler who would reform the Church. Others hoped not only for the 'renewal of the Church' (*renovatio ecclesiae*) but for the renewal of the world itself. In the fifteenth century, these expectations crystallized on the figure of Charles's great-grandfather the emperor Frederick III. The idea of universal empire was neatly expressed in his motto, AEIOU, with its double meaning in Latin and German, 'Austria will rule the world' (*Austria Est Imperare Orbe Universo*) or 'the whole world is subject to Austria' (*Alles Erdreich Ist Oesterreich Untertan*).

At the beginning of the sixteenth century, Frederick's son and successor Maximilian (according to the German astrologer Johan Lichtenberger) and Charles VIII of France (according to the Italian preacher fra Girolamo Savonarola) were both expected to fulfill the prophecies. A messianic tradition of this kind also developed around the kings of Aragon in the late Middle Ages. The events of 1492, the conquest of Granada and the conversion of the 'Moors' as well as the discovery of the New World, encouraged this tradition to crystallize around the figure of Ferdinand the Catholic. With his mixed ancestry, Charles stood at the confluence of Spanish and Germanic expectations of a universal monarchy.

The imperial image was constructed not only from grand expectations like these, but out of tiny details the significance of which is easy to miss in a later and especially a less formal age like our own. For example, the modes of address employed in letters to and from Charles offer a number of valuable clues to general changes over time in both the self-image of the emperor and the views which others took of him. When he first appeared on the political stage, Charles presented himself in a humble manner. In 1515, for instance, he wrote to Francis I to congratulate him on the victory of Marignano, calling him his 'good father' (*Monsieur mon bon père*) and signing 'Your humble son and vassal (*Votre humble fils et vassal*)'. The survival into the sixteenth century of the feudal language of 'vassal' is worth noting.

Later in the reign, as the emperor became an adult, the king of France was demoted from father to brother (*Monsieur mon bon frère*), though Charles continued to present himself to the popes as a 'humble son' (*fils très humble*, or *humilde hijo*), the verbal equivalent of the gesture of kissing the pope's foot which Charles performed in public on more than one occasion. On the other hand, other people increasingly humbled themselves to him. His brother Ferdinand signed letters to Charles 'your most humble and obedient brother' (*très humble et très obéissant frère*), or 'your most humble brother and servant, obedient like a son to a father' (*très humble frère, serviteur et obeissant comme filz au père*), while his sister Mary of Hungary called herself 'your most humble and most obedient sister and servant (*très humble et très obéissant soeur et servante*)'. High officials of state such as Cobos went still further, signing 'your most humble vassal and servant (*très humble vassal et serviteur or su mas humilde vasallo y fiel criado*)' or even 'slave and servant (*esclave et serviteur*)', sometimes adding for good measure 'I kiss your royal feet and hands' (*beso sus reales pies y manos*).

The official titles of the emperor also reflected his increasing grandeur. In 1515, when he made his state visit to Bruges, he was styled 'Charles, Prince of the Spains' (*Charles, Prince des Espagnes*). At Frankfurt, on 28 June 1519, he became 'King of the Romans, elected emperor, always august'. On 5 December 1520, it was officially announced that Charles was to be addressed as 'Sacra, Cesárea, Católica, Real Majestad' (sometimes abbreviated for convenience to SCCRM). Charles was King of the Romans, Spain (or the Spains, in other words Castille, Aragon, Navarre, and Granada), Sicily, Jerusalem, the Balearic Islands, Hungary, Dalmatia, Croatia, and the Indies. He was also Archduke of Austria; Duke of Burgundy, Brabant, Styria, Carinthia, Carniola, Luxemburg, Limburg, Athens and Patras; Count of Habsburg, Flanders and Tyrol; Count Palatine of Burgundy, Hainault, Pfirt, and Roussillon; Landgrave of Alsace, Count of Swabia, and so on. The full list of his titles was impressive indeed, including references to four continents, since Charles was styled 'Lord in Asia and Africa' as well as King of the Indies. The length of the list was an important part of the message.

However, these titles, like the many quarterings which Charles had a right to display, were not always used in full. The list was fluid rather than standardized and it fluctuated according to the demands of the occasion. In the text of the treaty of Bologna of 1529, for example, the emperor was styled 'unconquered (*invictissimus*)', but not in treaties with Francis I, probably in order not to offend the king at whose expense some of the victories had taken place. For certain purposes the list of titles was abbreviated. On coins, for example, Charles became 'Charles by the Grace of God Emperor of the Romans, King of Spain, Duke of Burgundy (CAROLUS. D. G. ROM. IMP. HISP. REX. DUX. BURG.)' On the other hand, the imperial letter to the Shah of Persia sent in 1525 in view of a possible alliance against the Ottoman sultan, was treated as a special occasion, marked as such by extra titles such as 'emperor of the Christian world (*christiani orbis imperator*)' and king of `the Indies, the new and gold-bearing world (*Indiarum novique et auriferi orbis*)'.

Many admiring epithets were applied to the emperor, as they had been to his predecessors, and a number of them recur throughout the reign. 'Divine (*Divus*)' is a good example of classically-flavoured humanist hyperbole, and it should not be taken to mean that Charles's subjects had been converted to pagan emperor-worship. 'Unconquered', or more literally 'most unconquered' (*Invictíssimo*)' occurs in the early 1520s, at a time when few battles had yet been fought in the emperor's name. The Italian bishop Giovanni Della Casa also referred to Charles's 'unconquered and unconquerable spirit (*invitto e invincibile animo*). If 'triumphant' was not a common epithet, the command 'let him triumph' (*triumphet*) occurs on a medal of 1545, and there were many references to specific triumphs, notably by the Spanish poet Vasco Diaz Tanco in his description of the coronation at Bologna. Still stronger was the language of 'taming', as in the case of a medal by Hans Schwarz, struck in 1521 and describing Charles as 'TAMER OF THE FRENCH AND THE SWISS' (*FRANCOR. ET HELVETOR. DOMITOR*).

The message was reinforced visually by showing the emperor crowned with laurel, or with a defeated enemy at his feet, as in the equestrian portrait by Vermeyen. It took an unusually ambitious form in the image of 'The Submission of all Princes to Charles V', the climax of a series of engravings of imperial victories published in 1556, in which Charles sits enthroned in the centre of the print, flanked by six defeated rulers. On the emperor's right stand Suleiman the Magnificent, pope Clement

VII and Francis I, while on his left hand we see the defeated Protestant princes, Wilhelm of Cleves, Johan Frederick of Saxony, and Philip of Hesse.

The emperor was also presented as a prince of peace: the inscription on an arch erected for his entry into Rome in 1536 describes him as PACIFICUS, while a medal struck to commemorate the peace of Cambrai, is dedicated 'to the peacemaker (FUNDATORI QUIETIS). The emperor's magnanimity (*magnitudo animi*) was mentioned by Gattinara and described by the official historians Juan Ginés de Sepúlveda (c. 1490-1573) and Luis de Avila y Zúñiga (1500-64), while the Italian poet Ludovico Ariosto described him as 'the magnanimous Charles (*il magnanimo Carlo*)'. His calm or *gravitas* was also emphasised. Charles was also 'pious' (*Carolus ille pius*, on the inscription on a medal struck in 1545); 'successful' (*felix*), the epithet traditionally applied to the ancient Roman leader Sulla; 'clement'; 'just'; and 'liberal' (although an outsider, the Venetian ambassador Nicolò Tiepolo, commented specifically on Charles's lack of 'liberality and magnificence'). In short, the emperor was 'Great' or even 'the Greatest' (*Magnus* or *Maximus*). He was sometimes described on the classical Roman model as 'the father of his country (*pater patriae*)'.

An analysis of the language of official documents reveals a good deal about the way in which Charles saw himself, or how he was perceived by the officials in his entourage, or how they wanted him to be perceived by a wider public. For example, there was the legal language of imperial rights and prerogatives, a language of property describing Charles as `true owner and sovereign lord' (*vrai propriétaire et souverain seigneur*), and speaking of his `full' or even 'absolute' power (*puissance plainière et absolue*). There was the rhetoric of the public good, with references to the *bien public* or *bien commun*, or to the emperor as sensitive to 'the oppression of the poor people' (*oppression du povre peuple*). There was the religious language in which Charles referred to God's help (*l'aide de Dieu*), or to God as taking his side (*favoreciendo nuestra causa*), at the battle of Pavia, for example, describing 'the imperial dignity' as one 'which our said creator has given us' (*la dignité impériale, en laquelle nostredit createur nous a mis*).

A few main messages or images recur in the media, four in particular: the emperor as overlord, as knight, as crusader and as the head of a dynasty. In the first place, then, there was the reiteration of the common medieval view that the emperor ruled the whole of Europe, at least in an indirect manner. Charles was, as the bishop of Badajoz put it in a speech of 1520, 'more king than any other' (*mas Rey que otro*), because he possessed more kingdoms and also because he was a 'king of kings'.

In the second place, the emperor was frequently presented as a heroic knight, an image which Titian captured with great skill in his marvellous equestrian portrait, but one which goes back at least as far as Hans Daucher's stone relief of 1522 in which Charles in armour controls his rearing charger. This image was of course reminiscent of the chivalric self-presentation of Charles's grandfather Maximilian. Indeed, it is surely Charles rather than Maximilian who should be described as 'the last knight' (*Der letzte Ritter*). His devotion to the values of chivalry was expressed by his apparent willingness to meet his opponent Francis in single combat, a challenge issued in 1526, following the French king's breach of his promise to return to captivity in Spain and Charles's declaration to the French ambassador that

Francis had acted 'in a cowardly and base manner' (*lachement et méchantement*). The challenge was repeated in 1528 and 1536. The combat never took place, which may have been just as well for the emperor, since Charles had rather less experience of fighting than his adversary. Whether or not it was meant seriously, the challenge ought to be viewed as an important media event, an inspired piece of political theatre which impressed contemporaries and posterity alike.

In the third place, Charles was both presented and represented as the defender of the faith and of the church (*protector et defensor ecclesiae*). In this respect he was the true heir of the Spanish tradition of the 'Catholic kings', the crusader first against the Turks and later against the Protestants. At his coronation, he swore to defend the church. This role of defender was symbolized by the emperor's sword of state, which was carried before him on special occasions. It was reaffirmed in the allegorical portrait of Charles as St James of Spain – if this is the correct identification – since the saint was traditionally nicknamed 'Kill Moors' (*Matamoros*), a reference to the legend that the saint had come to the assistance of the Spanish Christians in a battle with the Muslims at Clavijo in the year 844.

It is clear that a number of the emperor's subjects both wanted and expected him to play the role of defender of the faith, the 'secular arm' of the Church against the infidel (*bras seculier contre les infidelles*) as the herald Nicaise Ladam described him in 1519. In a speech delivered at Molins de Rey near Barcelona in November 1519, for example, Gattinara declared that Charles would recover the Holy Land. At the Cortes of 1520, the bishop of Badajoz declared that the emperor would devote his life to the defence of the faith. In 1529, the humanist Sepúlveda exhorted Charles to undertake a crusade against the Turks, emphasizing the danger to the 'Christian commonwealth' following the recent fall of Buda to the forces of Suleiman the Magnificent. In 1530, the papal legate Lorenzo Campeggio made the same point in his oration at the Diet of Augsburg. The emperor's former confessor Fernando García de Loaysa (c. 1480-1546) wrote to him in 1532, reproaching him for not having yet taken action against the Turks. The Tunis campaign (below) was long expected. Playing on these expectations, Charles's coins carried the exhortation, addressed to God, 'Give me strength against your enemies' (*DA. MIHI. VIRTUTE[M]. CO[NTRA]. HOSTES. TUOS*). As we have seen, treaties employed the idea of Charles as defender of the faith to justify his policies in Europe. Against this political background the equestrian portrait by Titian may be taken to represent Charles not only as a knight but more specifically as a crusader.

In the fourth place, Charles was viewed as the representative of the Habsburg dynasty, the descendant as well as the successor of a number of emperors. The official chronicler Pedro Mexia found it natural to begin his history of the emperor's reign with Charles's ancestors. For his state entry into Naples, the images of four such ancestors were displayed, the emperors Sigismund, Albert, Frederick and Maximilian. References to the Archduke Rudolf, who became the first Habsburg emperor in 1262, were commonplace. Charles's descent from the crusader Godfrey of Bouillon was also noted on occasion. Like his claim to the Kingdom of Jerusalem, of which Godfrey had been the first ruler, Charles's genealogical tree supported the idea of an imperial crusade.

Charles was also viewed as the descendant of `the invincible Gothic kings (*los invencibles reyes godos*)', as they were called by Pedro Mexia, in other words the Visigoth conquerors of Spain. Like the Swedes, the Spaniards (or some of them at any rate), gloried in these barbarian ancestors. As the emperor himself remarked on one occasion, `we too are of Gothic ancestry (*et nos de gente Gothorum sumus*)'. Going back still further, as many genealogists liked to do at this time, the emperor's descent from Hector of Troy was mentioned by Ariosto. His descent from Noah was affirmed by the Alsatian humanist Hieronymus Gebweiler in his *Epitome regii ortus* (1530), and by the papal notary Pietro Mareno in his *Compendio delle Stirpe di Carlo Magno et Carlo V* (1545).

Charles was frequently glorified by means of favourable comparisons with heroic rulers from the past. Among these parallels one of the most frequent was the comparison with Charlemagne. Prophecies of a second Charlemagne had been in circulation for centuries, often linked to the hope in the coming of the Last World Emperor, discussed above. When a youth with the name of Charles was elected Holy Roman Emperor in 1519, the rapid fulfillment of the prophecy seemed all the more plausible. Charles was not only a namesake but also a successor of Charlemagne, a point underlined by his coronation in Charlemagne's capital, Aachen. On this occasion Charles sat on Charlemagne's throne, while the head of his illustrious predecessor was carried in procession.

The dedication of a new edition of a life of Charlemagne written in the ninth century by the monk Einhard, published in Cologne in 1521, took the opportunity to compare the two emperors, and the titlepage illustration showed them together. The Bologna entry of 1530 made the same point (below). Ariosto's *Orlando Furioso*, a story which was set in the time of Charlemagne, included in its revised version of 1532 a prophecy of the future greatness of Charles V in deliberate imitation or emulation of the prophecy concerning Augustus in the sixth book of Virgil's *Aeneid*. In more prosaic fashion, in his *Compendio delle Stirpe di Carlo Magno et Carlo V imperatori* (1545), the apostolic protonotary Pietro Mareno discussed the relationship between the two rulers.

The climax of these comparisons was reached in a prolix panegyric published in 1559 by Guillaume Snouckaert van Schouwenburg (or as he styled himself in Latin, Zenocarus a Scauwenburgo, 1518-65). Snouckaert, a jurisconsult from Ghent who held the office of librarian to the emperor, noted no fewer than thirty-nine points of comparison between the two rulers in his *De republica, vita, moribus, gestis, fama, religione, sanctitate: Imperatoris, Caesaris, Augusti, Quinti, Caroli, Maximi, Monarchae, Libri VII*.

In the sixteenth century it was fashionable for a prince like other nobles to adopt a personal device or *impresa*, combining an image with a motto. Charles's device, adopted by 1516, consisted of two columns, representing the pillars of Hercules, together with the phrase 'still further' (*plus ultra, plus oultre, noch weiter* etc). The *impresa* could be seen everywhere in the emperor's dominions: on the reverse of coins, on tapestries, on walls, on the titlepages of books, on the sail of Charles's flagship, and so on. Whether or not it originally referred to the discovery of the New World, the device was certainly a declaration of Charles's intent to outdo Charlemagne, whose empire, like that of the ancient Romans, had been bounded by the pillars of Hercules (a poetic way of describing the Straits of Gibraltar).

The idea that if Charlemagne was 'great' (*magnus*), Charles was the greatest' (*maximus*) became a commonplace. Used as early as 1519 in a congratulatory speech by the German diplomat Bernhard Wurmser, it was employed in the 1520s by Valdés. In similar vein, in his *History of his own time*, the Italian humanist bishop Paolo Giovio commented on the battle of Mühlberg that 'If Charlemagne, who had struggled in Saxony for thirty years, deserved the title of "Great", then Charles V certainly ought to be called more than "Greatest" on triumphal arches, for having tamed and defeated the Saxons in fewer than thirty weeks (*se Carlo Magno, avendo stentato trenta anni in questa Sassonia, meritò il cognome di Magno, certamente per questa ragione Carlo Quinto, poi che in meno di trenta settimana l'ha domata e sconfitta, doverà essere appellata più che Massimo nelli archi triunfali*).'

Charles was also viewed as a second version of a number of ancient heroes, historical or mythological – a distinction made less systematically and less clearly in the emperor's time than it would be in the nineteenth and twentieth centuries. Three Old Testament heroes in particular were mentioned in this context. According to Cardinal Egidio da Viterbo (1469-1532), for instance, the emperor was a new Moses, leading the human race towards liberty. According to Peter of Ghent, in a manuscript called *Salomonis officia*, now in the Escorial, he was a new Solomon. According to Eberhard van der Mark, prince-bishop of Liège and author of 'The Deeds of Charles V (*Gesta Caroli Quinti*), the emperor was a new David. Charles was even compared to Christ, notably in a sermon of 1556 preached by the Cistercian monk Cipriano de Huerga which referred to Charles as the good shepherd.

Classical parallels with the emperor were more frequent. Thanks to his many conquests, the emperor was viewed as a modern version of Alexander the Great. Like Charles VIII of France, he was described as a new Cyrus, the king of Persia who was the hero of Xenophon's *Cyropaedia*. His exploits in North Africa led Charles to be presented as a new Scipio, with medals and portraits describing him, like Scipio, with the honorific title of 'Africanus'. With his customary overkill, Snouckaert also compared the emperor to Pompey, Sulla, Fabius Maximus and Hannibal. Given his title 'Caesar' it was of course inevitable that Charles would be viewed as a new Julius Caesar (a comparison to which Snouckaert devoted no fewer than three pages). It was to evoke his memory that both Charles's memoirs and a number of histories of his reign were described as 'commentaries', the word that Julius Caesar had used to describe his own accounts of his wars. The emperor was also described as a new Augustus, in whose time the golden age would return together with Astraea the goddess of justice. The prophecy was made in the fifteenth canto of Ariosto's Orlando Furioso, once again echoing Virgil's *Aeneid*, and it was illustrated soon afterwards in the decorative programme for the emperor's entry into the city of Messina in 1535.

The Christian emperor was also described as a new Constantine, and – by the Italian nobleman, scholar and poet Giangiorgio Trissino (1478-1550), in 1547 – as a new Justinian. According to Antonio de Guevara, Charles was both a new Marcus Aurelius and a new Trajan. Indeed, Guevara went so far as to invent an expedition of Trajan to North Africa as a precedent for Charles's expedition to Tunis. The emperor was of course supposed to have surpassed all these predecessors.

A bust of Charles, displayed at the hospital of San Marcos in León, described him as 'better than Trajan, more successful than Augustus (*Melior Trajano, Felicior Augusto*)'.

Like ancient history, classical mythology was raided for parallels which would glorify the emperor. For example, in a speech by Luigi Marliani (d. 1521), an Italian humanist bishop who doubled as Charles's physician, to the chapter of the Order of the Golden Fleece in 1516, Charles was described as a new Atlas, carrying the world on his shoulders. The comparison would recur at the time of the emperor's abdication, when the burden had become too heavy for him to bear and Prince Philip was represented giving him aid. Charles was a new Jupiter, ruling the world below as Jupiter ruled the heavens, as in the Antwerp entry of 1520 which described the emperor as *alter Juppiter* and also applied to him the traditional epithets of that god, 'the best and the greatest' (*Optimus Maximus*). Giulio Romano's frescoes at the Palazzo del Te in Mantua representing Jupiter with thunderbolts, and painted around the time of Charles's visit to Italy in 1530, have often been taken to refer to the emperor. The image recurs in the Naples entry of 1536, and there would be further recourse to this image of the emperor in 1547 (below).

Charles was sometimes described as a new Jason, a reference to the Burgundian chivalric Order of the Golden Fleece, of which he was the head. More often he was a 'new Hercules', as in Marliani's speech, in a Latin poem by the Portuguese humanist Damião de Gois, and on a medal designed by the Italian sculptor Leone Leoni. The comparison was also made in the Florence entry in 1536, which represented Hercules in combat with the hydra (a symbol of disorder or heresy), at the bridge of Santa Trinità, and again in the Paris entry of 1540, when the emperor was presented with a life-size silver statue of Hercules. Charles's device of the Pillars of Hercules made this comparison especially appropriate. In any case, Hercules was traditionally supposed to have been one of the ancestors of the kings of Spain.

Charles was also described and represented as the eagle mentioned by the prophet Ezekiel, 'A great eagle with great wings ... full of feathers, which had diverse colours' (*Ezechiel* 17, 3), echoed in the late medieval prophecies of St Bridget of Sweden. The application of the prophecy to Charles was encouraged by the symbol of the double-headed eagle in the Habsburg coat of arms. To this effect, around the year 1543, the Italian Euralio d'Ascoli wrote a poem called 'The Device of the Eagle (*Impresa dell'aquila*), the illustrated manuscript of which is still to be found in Vienna. By contrast, Charles's adversary Francis was presented by apologists for the Habsburgs as a less noble bird, proud and boastful, either a cock or a peacock. Like some Roman emperors, not to mention Kings Philip IV of Spain and Louis XIV of France in the next century, Charles was sometimes compared to the sun, notably in a panegyric by one of his confessors, Juan Cristóbal Calvete de la Estrella. The sun-king Louis XIV was far from the first to be described in these terms.

More common was the idea of Charles as world emperor or universal shepherd, a role symbolized by the imperial orb or *pomus rotundus*, the significance of which was discussed by lawyers such as Restaurus Castaldus of Perugia. Modern historians sometimes translate the term 'world (*orbis, mundo, mondo* etc)' as 'Christendom', arguing – as the Spanish historian Juan Antonio Maravall has done – that the idea of universal monarchy must not be taken in 'too literal a sense'. This revision is surely misleading. It was a maxim of Roman law that, as the fourteenth-century jurist Bartolus of Sassoferrato phrased it, 'the emperor is legally lord of the whole world' (*imperator de iure est dominus totius orbis*). Sixteenth-century civil lawyers such as Castaldus or Miguel Ulçurrun of Pamplona discussed whether the emperor had received his world rulership directly from God or whether he was simply the substitute or 'vicar' of the pope (Ulçurrun argued that the pope was merely head of the faithful, while the emperor was head of the infidels as well). The idea of universal monarchy was expressed in a number of different phrases (among them *imperium mundi, regimen mundi,* and *potestas universalis in orbe*).

These phrases were applied to different rulers (to Francis I in France, for example), and they appear to have meant different things to different people, being taken more or less literally or metaphorically according to the contexts. The lawyers, for example, sometimes appear to have been discussing a rather vague kind of overlordship including the right to be consulted, and they sometimes used the vague formulation *moderator orbis*. However, given the fact that the emperor had inherited authority over a remarkable amount of the earth's surface, it is hardly surprising that some people thought of him as a world ruler in a more direct sense, whether in the present or in the future – his confessor Loaysa wrote to Charles that he expected him to become 'the true and absolute lord of the world' (*verdadero y absoluto señor del mundo*).

In some cases, this image had negative associations, suggesting a tyrant with a passion for power (*libido dominandi*) who wanted to reduce his subjects to servitude. Between the mid-sixteenth and mid-seventeenth centuries, the desire for universal monarchy in this negative sense would come to be associated with the rulers of Spain in particular.

How many people hoped – or feared – that Charles would rule the whole world is impossible to say, but it is worth remembering that the millennium was widely expected around the year 1500. The forced conversion of the Jews and Muslims in the Iberian peninsula following the capture of Granada in 1492 was recent memory. The conversion of the American Indians had begun. The imminent defeat of the Ottoman sultan was expected. Thus the prophecy of one flock and one shepherd appeared to be on the verge of fulfillment in Charles's time. His confessor Loaysa wrote to him in 1531 that he expected the emperor 'to fulfill the ancient prophecies which speak of your monarchy' (*cumplir los pronosticos antiguos que hablan de vuestra monarchia*), and 'to finish off the Ottoman dynasty' (*dar fin a esta casa de Turco*).

There were therefore apparently good grounds for taking the idea of universal monarchy quite seriously, whether one approved of it or not. In a sermon before the chapter of the Order of the Golden Fleece in 1516, Marliani spoke about this world empire when he suggested that Charles adopt the 'plus ultra' device. Again, the diplomat Bernhard Wurmser, in his oration to Charles congratulating him on his election as emperor in 1519, addressed him as 'the true and most powerful ruler of the world' (*verum ac potissimum orbis dominatorem*), and 'king of kings' (*Regem regum*). That the idea was also taken seriously by statesmen is apparent in chancellor Gattinara's famous memorial to the emperor of 12 July 1519, written a few weeks after his election.

On this occasion Gattinara told his master that God had been very merciful to him, making him 'the greatest emperor and king there has been (*le plus grand empereur et roy qui ayt este*)' since the division of the empire by Charlemagne, 'setting you on the right road of monarchy, to unite the whole world under a single shepherd (*vous dressant au droit chemin de la monarchie pour reduire l'universel monde soubz ung pasteur*)'. A newly-discovered manuscript by Gattinara, 'On the new world monarchy and the future triumph of the Christians (*De novissima orbis monarchia ac futuro christianorum triumpho*)', written during his temporary retirement to a monastery in 1516-17, went still further and presents Charles (to whom the manuscript was dedicated) as the last world emperor.

The theme of the universal shepherd reverberated through the reign and was expressed in public statements as well as Gattinara's private memoranda to the emperor. In 1520, for example, the Antwerp entry included an inscription with the prophecy 'There will be one flock on earth and one shepherd (Grex unus terris pastor et unus erit)'. The commentary on the Apocalypse of St John published in 1524 by the Franciscan Petrus Galatinus and dedicated to the emperor, referred to the coming age of one shepherd, one flock, one law and one prince and identified Charles as the Last World Emperor. The Seville entry of 1526, on the occasion of Charles's wedding, included a triumphal arch inscribed 'Charles the greatest now rules the whole world (*Maximus in toto regnat nunc Carolus orbe*). In the Genoa entry of 1529, a choir hailed Charles as 're del mondo', and the image of an eagle on a globe was prominently displayed.

The traditional links between the world emperor, the defender of the faith and the reform of the Church were not forgotten. In the age of Luther, it was especially tempting to view Charles as the long-expected agent of the 'Renewal of the Church', particularly when he threatened the pope with a general council and when his army sacked Rome.

The iconography of the famous portrait of Charles with a globe by Parmigianino, dating from 1530, made the same point. So did Ariosto's *Orlando Furioso* in its revised version published two years later, with its claim that God 'wishes there to be only one flock and one shepherd in the time of this emperor (*vuol che sotto a questo imperatore/solo un ovile sia, solo un pastore)*'. The engraved terrestrial globe which the humanist geographer Gemma Frisius dedicated to Charles in 1535 was another visual assertion of world domination – not to mention a specific claim in the dispute over the Moluccas, islands claimed not only by the emperor but also by King João III of Portugal. The decorations for Charles's state entry into the city of Messina in 1535 included an image of the emperor standing on a revolving globe. Again, a German translation of the fifth-century text by Orosius (discussed above), published in 1539, inserted a reference to Charles V into the account of the succession of world empires. A medal of Charles by Leone Leoni carries the inscription 'MONARCH OF THE WORLD' (*MONARCA DEL MONDO*). The same medal refers to the 'Renovation of the World', a hope which had once been associated with ancient Roman emperors.

The most famous expression of this idea, however, is the sonnet written by the soldier poet Hernando de Acuña and addressed to Charles around the year 1547: 'The glorious age is at hand, Sir, if it has not arrived already, in which Heaven promises that there shall be only one flock and one shepherd on earth, a destiny reserved for your times'. (*Ya se acerca, señor, o ya es llegada/la edad gloriosa en que promete el cielo/una grey y un pastor solo en el suelo/por suerte a vuestros tiempos reservada*). A variation on this theme was provided by the Franciscan friar Toríbio de Benavente, known as 'Motolínia', a missionary in the New World, when he wrote to the emperor in 1555 describing him as 'the leader and captain' (*caudillo y capitan*) of 'the Fifth Monarchy of Jesus Christ (*el quinto reino de Jesu-Cristo*),' which would occupy the whole earth before the end of the world (*la consumación del mundo*). According to this letter, Charles was destined to fulfill the prophecy in the Book of Daniel in which the image of an idol with a golden head and feet of clay represented the four successive monarchies of the Assyrians, Medes, Persians and Romans. Motolínia was among those who interpreted the conversion of the Indians in the New World as a sign that the millennium was at hand.

As the examples discussed above suggest, the emperor's career offers an unusually clear example of what might be called the 'mythification' of an individual in his own time, defining the slippery term 'myth' in terms of three criteria. In the first place, a myth may be described as a story of marvellous or extra-ordinary events in which the protagonists are larger than life, endowed with superhuman qualities, whether they are heroes or villains. Indeed these protagonists represent, embody or symbolize values, making abstract ideas concrete and so more memorable. In the second place, from a structural point of view, a myth may be viewed as a story composed of schemata, in other words recurrent or prefabricated elements which wander or float from one story or one protagonist to another. In the third place, from a functional point of view, a myth may be regarded as a story about the past the purpose of which is to legitimate a situation or an institution in the present.

The emperor was certainly presented as larger than life, as the many parallels between Charles and past heroes should have made abundantly clear. His reign was described by Pedro Mexía, in the introduction to his officially-commissioned *Historia de Carlos Quinto*, as a time of 'great deeds and marvellous events in war and peace, which have happened by his efforts or at his orders (*grandes hechos y cosas maravillosas de guerra y paz, que por el o por su mandado han sido*)'.

Not everyone was as careful as Mexia to make this distinction between Charles's direct and indirect responsibility for the events of his reign. The title 'Carolina' reminds us that Charles was officially presented as responsible for a new code of laws for the Empire, although the code was in fact drawn up by professional lawyers and Charles had nothing whatever to do with it. How literally this myth of imperial agency was taken at the time, whether in the field of war or in that of law, it is difficult to say. The problem is a recurrent one. One of the main ways in which myth works is by condensing and personifying the historical process. Like Atlas carrying the world on his shoulders, a few heroic individuals are made to bear the whole weight of responsibility for the events of their time.

So far the description and analysis of the imperial image has been a thematic one. Such a description has the advantage of clarity, but at the price of presenting a static picture. In compensation, the following section will tell a story, or more exactly it will present a moving picture of the emperor over his long reign.

The deeds of the emperor

The purpose of this section is to offer a brief history of Charles's reign viewed from the angle of the construction and the stage-management of the imperial image. A relatively brief account must inevitably be highly selective. In what follows I shall privilege seven major events or clusters of events This imperial drama in seven acts focusses in turn on Charles's election and coronation at Aachen; his conflicts with François I at the time of the battle of Pavia; his conflicts with Clement VII and the Sack of Rome; his coronation at Bologna; the Tunis campaign; the campaign against the Protestant princes; and finally the emperor's abdication, retirement and death. In this section, unlike the previous one, it seems appropriate to speak of 'propaganda', despite the fact that the term was not yet in use, because it allows a distinction to be drawn between generalized panegyric of the kind already discussed and attempts to impose an official interpretation on specific events.

1. Election and Coronation

Charles's election as emperor in 1519 and his first coronation in 1520 may be considered not only as rites of passage for the protagonist but also, from the public's point of view, as public statements of his imperial identity. Despite the lack of time for preparation, there is evidence of the use of what might be called `propaganda' in the campaign on Charles's behalf. The young prince was of course untested and indeed virtually unknown at this time, so the technique adopted by his supporters (organized by Margaret of Austria) was to emphasise his German ancestry (in contrast to his main rival, Francis I) and his enthusiasm for making war on the Turks. Attempts were made to stir up anti-French feelings and to present Francis as a threat to the liberties of the nobles and cities of the Empire. To assess the importance of this propaganda relative to the gifts and promises to the electors is obviously impossible, but at any rate, Charles was successful.

The coronation of Charles as King of the Romans took place in traditional style in the cathedral of Aachen. He had been met outside the city by four of the seven electors, and there was an elaborate exchange of courtesies in which Charles tried to dismount and one of the electors tried to prevent him from doing so. There was a procession to the cathedral in which the Count Palatine carried Charles's sword, money was thrown to the crowd, while trumpets and drums sounded. At the ceremony itself, the archbishop of Cologne officiated. The emperor took an oath to defend the church, justice, widows and so on. He was solemnly vested with the pallium, alb, and stole, and with the imperial insignia of sword, ring, sceptre and crown. Following the coronation the emperor sat on Charlemagne's throne, while some of his subjects kissed his knee. He also created a number of knights and participated in a banquet. An American scholar, Karl Morrison, has called for an 'anthropological analysis of Charles's coronation', viewing it as 'a vestigial remnant of medieval Germany'. It certainly followed medieval traditions. On the other hand, the style of later presentations and representations of the emperor may be described as approaching a Renaissance or classical model more and more closely in the course of the reign.

News of the coronation arrived in Brussels on 30 June, two days after it had taken place, and on the orders of Margaret of Austria the happy event was immediately celebrated with bonfires in the streets. News-sheets in various languages informed Europe of what had happened. The German humanist Heinrich Cornelius Agrippa, Hermann Mohr, professor of law at university of Cologne and counsellor to the Archbishop, the herald Nicaise Ladam, author of *Le joyeux reveil de l'election imperiale de Prince Charles*, and the Swiss printer Pamphilus Gengenbach, later well-known as a Protestant propagandist, were among those who published descriptions of the imperial election and coronation. The description in the form of a letter by the humanist Giovanni Antonio Flaminio was printed in 1530. Printed prophecies about Charles also circulated at time of his election, together with calls for a universal monarchy. The prophecy of Alofresant of Rhodes, for example, entitled the *Keyserliche Practica und Prognostication*, published in 1519, and reprinted in French at Antwerp c. 1528 as the *Prophesies du tresnoble, trespuissant et tresexcellent Empereur Charles*, declared that Charles would rule 'from east to west' (*von Orient bis in Occident*). Berthold Purstinger also published prophecies about Charles in his *Onus Ecclesiae*, 1519.

2. Habsburg versus Valois

The second act of the drama is dominated by the conflict between Charles and the King of France, Francis I, together with his ally the pope, Clement VII. This cluster of events includes the battle of Pavia, the Treaty of Madrid, and the sack of Rome (1525-7). The emperor's own view of these events in later life, as it emerges from the laconic prose of his memoirs, emphasises the 'exorbitant demands' of Francis (*requerimentos ... exorbitantes*), and his sense of affront when the pope intervened in the dispute, especially what Charles described as the papal legate's lack of 'respect'.

The battle of Pavia, in which the king of France was captured, was naturally a major news item of the time. The *Relación de las nuevas de Italia* (which describes the battle in detail) ends with a colophon which shows that the government had been taking advantage of this unusual propaganda opportunity: 'The Lords of the Council ... ordered me, Alonso de Valdes ... to have the present account printed (*Los señores del consejo ... mandaron a mi Alonso de Valdes ... que fiziesse imprimir la presente relación)*'. Valdés claimed that the victory was a 'miraculous' one, given by God in order that Charles would be in a position to attack the Turk, who was threatening to invade Italy, and also to recover Constantinople and Jerusalem.

Like Charles's election, the victory was presented as the fulfillment of prophecy. Visual images of the battle of Pavia, drawing attention to the capture of the King of France, also abounded, including Orley's design for a tapestry, woodcuts by Georg Breu and Hans Schäufelein, and a painting by the Dutch artist Martin Heemskerck (1498-1574), engraved by another Dutchman, Dirck Coornhert (1522-90), giving the battle a place in what had become by the end of the reign the canonical series of Charles's twelve victories.

The imperial historian Pedro Mexia described the battle of Pavia as 'one of the most violent battles in the history of the world (*una de las más bravas batallas del mundo)*', in which everyone fought like lions and there was so much noise of gunfire, fifes and trumpets that the earth seemed to tremble. The emperor was not present at the battle, unlike his opponent Francis I, but his reactions to the news of the victory were described by Mexia at some length as an example of Charles's famous gravity (*gravedad*). When the news arrived in Madrid, Charles 'did not show the slightest change of expression or attitude, nor did he say anything or show any kind of joy or pleasure (*no mostró en su gesto ni semblante la menor alteración del mundo, ni dijo palabra ni hizo muestra de plazer ni alegria alguna*)'. All he did was to give thanks to God. The humanist historian Sepúlveda made the same point more briefly.

Mexia also commented on the emperor's lack of vainglory and of the desire for vengeance, and declares that 'in none of his deeds and successes did he show the magnanimity and greatness of his spirit as much as in this one' (*en ninguno de sus hechos y successos el mostraro la magnanimidad y grandeza de su animo como en esta*). In other words, Charles behaved, or more exactly was presented as behaving, in accordance with the stoic ideal of constancy or tranquillity of mind which his preacher and counsellor Guevara would soon be recommending to him in his famous treatise 'The Dial of Princes' (*Reloj de Principes*).

After Francis I had been released from captivity on condition that he surrender Burgundy, a condition which once free he refused to meet, the conflict between the two monarchs was conducted in the media. Francis defended himself with an apologia, to which Charles replied. However, the paper war did not end there. The emperor's entourage mounted what the American historian John Headley has called an 'imperial propaganda campaign'. The novelty of this campaign, a systematic attempt to demonstrate in print that Francis and his ally pope Clement VII were both in the wrong, deserves to be emphasized. Printing with moveable type had been established for three-quarters of a century, but this was the first time that a ruler made use of the medium on this scale against another ruler. It is not impossible that the emperor's advisers had been impressed by the effective way in which Martin Luther had been using print to justify his position and build his movement in the previous five years or so.

Let us examine these exchanges in rather more detail. In June 1526, pope Clement VII wrote a letter to Charles in which he asserted that by allying himself with Francis he was acting in self-defence, since the emperor was disturbing the peace of Christendom. In July, Francis published his *Apologia*, explaining that the fundamental laws of his kingdom forbade him to alienate territory.

The imperial reply to the pope's letter was written by Charles's secretary Alonso de Valdés and read aloud in public in September 1526 at Granada, where Charles and his court were residing at the time. The reply, known as *Pro divo carolo*, an attack on the pope as well as a defence of the emperor, was handed over to the papal nuncio, Baldassare Castiglione, for formal presentation to the pope in Rome. The text, which `struck the authentic note of righteous indignation', as the German historian Karl Brandi observed, was later published in five European cities, Cologne, Mainz, Antwerp, Basel and Rome. The imperial privilege to the printer Johannes Schoeffer of Mainz, who was the official printer to Charles's chancery, recommended the volume to the attention not only of the aristocracy but of ordinary citizens as well. This was not, of course, a realistic expectation for a Latin tract, but a German translation was published at Leipzig in 1529.

A letter from the emperor (written this time by Gattinara) to the ambassadors of the 'holy league' between France and the papacy was also made public at this time. The emperor also wrote, in November 1526, to the princes of the Roman Empire about the treaty of Madrid – and given the fact that the letter was soon printed (in Alcalà and Antwerp in 1527), to a much wider public as well. The letter denounced the French king's breach of faith, his insulting apologia or 'invective', and the 'most pernicious arts of the French (*perniciosissimas Gallorum artes*). It contrasted the 'perfidy' of Francis with Charles's concern with Christendom and the defence of Hungary against the Ottoman Empire. To put the argument in context, it should be remembered that the decisive battle of Mohács had recently taken place, in August 1526. The Hungarian army had been virtually annihilated, King Louis II had been killed, and most of the kingdom had been conquered by the Turks.

In the course of the years 1527-9, texts written in the name of Charles explaining his conduct and criticizing that of Francis I and the pope were published in Latin, French, Flemish and Spanish, under titles such as *Responsio ad duo Clementis breves, Réponse du puissant et très-invict empereur Charles V sur les lettres du roi de France, Antworde Caroli des vijfsten op den brief des Conincx van Vranckrijke*, and – referring to the famous challenge to single combat – *El desafio de los reyes de Francia y Inglaterra al emperador con sus respuestas*, and *Réponse de la très sacrée Majesté impériale sur le cartel du deffiement et combat du roi de France*.

3. The Sack of Rome (1527)

The Sack of Rome by imperial troops in 1527 was another kind of response to the Holy League, which sent shock-waves through Christendom and made it necessary for the emperor's publicists to justify his position. Gattinara hesitated before advising Charles to write to the princes of Christendom telling them of his 'great displeasure' (*grand desplaisir*) and 'very great regret' (*très grand regret*) for what had happened. At about this time, Gattinara asked Erasmus to edit a new edition of Dante's treatise on monarchy (which placed the emperor above the pope), but the invitation met with a refusal. Hence the task of justifying Charles was given once more to Alonso de Valdés, who wrote to Erasmus in 1529 telling him that he had written a dialogue which drew on Erasmian ideas and would free the emperor from the responsibility for the Sack.

Valdés produced two dialogues in Spanish on the subject as well as writing Latin letters on the emperor's behalf. In the first piece, the *Diálogo de las cosas occurridas en Roma*, a conversation between Lactancio and an archdeacon, Valdés argued that 'the emperor is not to blame' (*el Emperador ninguna culpa tiene*) for what had happened and that he now had the opportunity to reform the church. Valdés thus linked the topical subject of church reform with the imperial mission and presented the sack of Rome, like earlier events in the imperial reign, as the fulfillment of prophecy. This text circulated in manuscript before it was printed –without any indication of place or date, though apparently in Italy in 1528 or thereabouts.

Valdés went on to write another dialogue in Spanish, *Mercurio y Carón* (c. 1529), the aim of which was, as he put it, 'to demonstrate the justice of the emperor (*manifestar la justicia del Emperador*).' In this dialogue, following classical models, the god Mercury is described as descending to the underworld in order to inform the boatman Charon about the new emperor, describing him as 'Carlo Máximo', 'because his virtues and his greatness have so well deserved it (*pues sus virtudes y grandezas tan bien lo tienen merecido*).' Since he did not wish to begin his reign with war, Mercury explains, Charles made peace with the King of France, 'having more respect for the common good than for his private interests (*teniendo más respecto al bien público que a su particular provecho*).' Francis is presented as the villain of the piece, disappointed at not having been elected emperor, and so looking for 'an opportunity to do him [Charles] harm (*oportunidad para hazerle mal*).' All the same, having captured Francis at Pavia, the emperor 'treated him with as much love and humanity as if he had been his own brother' (*lo trató con tanto amor y tanta humanidad como si fuere su proprio hermano*). Charon too calls Charles 'a truly christian prince' (*príncipe verdaderamente christiano*).

The text, the last shot in the propaganda campaign, was presumably intended for a Spanish rather than a European audience. Although Charles's reconciliation with pope Clement (at the peace of Barcelona, in June 1529), soon robbed the dialogue of its topicality, five printed editions of the text survive. Without indications of place or date, as in the case of the previous dialogue, these editions may well have been printed in the early 1540s, possibly in Naples, when Charles was once again in conflict with the papacy.

In any case, the sack of Rome, which Charles officially claimed to have regretted, continued to be celebrated in his lifetime. Two images out of the twelve engravings of Charles's *Victories*, designed by the Dutch artist Maarten van Heemskerck, are concerned with episodes from the Roman campaign, the capture of the city (emphasizing the death of Charles duke of Bourbon), and the siege of pope Clement in Castel St Angelo.

4. *The coronation at Bologna (1530)*

Gattinara had long been pressing Charles to go to Italy to be crowned. There had been a plan for the ceremony to take place in Rome (as in the case of Charlemagne's coronation in the year 800), but this idea was abandoned – memories of the sack of the city were too recent – and Bologna was chosen instead. The city was decorated in honour of Charles with triumphal arches in Renaissance style; equestrian statues of the ancient Roman heroes Camillus and Scipio; medallions of four Roman emperors (Caesar, Augustus, Vespasian and Trajan);and statues of Constantine and Charlemagne, evoking the similarities between the two coronations by popes of emperors named Charles. The form of the occasion was planned by the papal master of ceremonies, but the massive presence of the imperial army (including cannon) in the procession gives – and was doubtless intended to give – the impression that it was Charles who was in control.

The ritual was divided into two parts. On 22 February 1530, Charles was crowned king of the Lombards. After Mass had been celebrated the pope sat on his throne and Charles, kneeling before him, was solemnly crowned with the famous iron crown of Lombardy, still to be seen at Monza, and he was given (among other objects) a ring which signified his marriage to the kingdom. He was then solemnly proclaimed king to the sound of salvos of artillery, drums, and trumpets.

On 24 February, Charles was crowned Holy Roman Emperor in the church of San Petronio, wearing in turn his imperial robes (including a mantle bearing the imperial eagle), the clothing of a canon of St Peter's, including a rochet and a berretta, the tunic of a deacon and finally his imperial robes again. The pope said Mass and afterwards invested Charles with a sword, a sceptre and an orb. The church was richly decorated for the occasion with tapestries, especially in the neighbourhood of Charles's eagle-decorated throne. The proceedings followed the order of the papal ceremonial, despite the breach of precedent involved in crowning the emperor outside Rome. The church of San Petronio was adapted to look as much as possible like St Peter's, in order to disguise the break with tradition and to give the impression of the re-enactment of the coronation of Charlemagne or more recently that of Charles IV, who had also been crowned by a pope named Clement.

A Spanish broadside or *pliego* described how, after the ceremony, 'The emperor with the crown on his head and the sceptre and orb in his hands accompanied the pope (*el emperador con la corona en la cabeza y el sceptro y pomo en las manos va al lado del pontifice*)' and how 'out of reverence for Our Lord Jesus Christ ... he held the stirrup until the pope was in the saddle (*en reverencia de Nuestro Señor Jesus Cristo ... tiene el estribo hasta que el pontifice ha subido*)'. A pictorial record of the coronation procession in forty plates (reminiscent of some woodcuts made for Maximilian by Hans Burgkmair), was made by official artists, Robert Péril and Nicolaus Hogenberg.

A record of this kind had not been made in the case of the

coronation at Aachen, so the decision suggests an increasing awareness of publicity in the imperial entourage. Accounts of the coronation circulated in manuscript in the form of letters from eyewitnesses and books on the subject were published by the Italian humanist Girolamo Balbi, bishop of Gurk (1530), and by the German humanist Georg Sabinus (1544). Balbi's text was less concerned with the events of 24 February than with the theological, legal, and political significance of the insignia and the ceremony. His main argument, which did not endear him to the pope, was that the act of coronation did not change anything, the emperor having become emperor as soon as he was elected, so that the ritual was honorific rather than strictly necessary.

5. *The conquest of Tunis*

The conquest of Tunis was presented from the first as victorious crusade. It was officially declared to be a crusade by pope Paul III. It was also presented as such from the moment of Charles's pilgrimage to the shrine of the Virgin Mary at Montserrat in Catalonia before he sailed for Africa. The interpretation was confirmed by Charles's remark that 'the crucified Saviour shall be our captain'. Following his return to Italy, the emperor's successive entries into Palermo, Messina, Naples, Genoa, Rome, Siena, Florence and Lucca took on an even more triumphal quality than usual.

The imperial entries to Palermo and Messina, for instance, made references to the campaign. In Naples, a triumphal arch was erected that included a representation of a 'conquered Africa full of sadness'. In Rome, a gateway carried the inscription 'To the destroyer of the Turks' (*Turcarum Eversori*). At St Peter's, another inscription was displayed, dedicated to the man who made the Muslims turn pale with fear, (*Maumetarum paucri pallorique*). A triumphal arch was designed by the architect Antonio de San Gallo and decorated with a series of paintings of the 'Triumph of Africa', including the battle of La Goletta, the capture of Tunis, Charles releasing Christian captives, and the coronation of the new King of Tunis, the emperor's protégé. In Florence, where duke Alessandro de' Medici put Giorgio Vasari in charge of the display, Charles was described as 'The Tamer of Africa' (*Domitor Africae*). Painted scenes represented the flight of the Turks, the coronation of the king of Tunis and the river Bagradas.

These displays were soon taken down, but other images of the campaign were more permanent. Newsheets in Italian (*La felice victoria de Tunisi*) and German (*Eroberung des Königreichs Tunisi*) appeared in print the same year. So did letters written in Charles's name to Maria of Hungary and to the imperial ambassador in France informing them of the victory, advertised as *Copie des lettres par l'impériale majesté à la douagière de Hongrie* (published in Bruges), and *Copie des lettres par l'impériale majesté à M. de Linkerke ambassadeur en France* (published in Antwerp).

Individuals added their own accounts of these events. The poem by the shoemaker Hans Sachs of Nuremberg, for instance, emphasized the fact that the emperor had gone to Africa in person (*mit eigner Person*), that he released Christian captives and that he converted many heathen (*viel unglaubig zum glauben bracht*). Antoine Perrenin, (died c. 1541), secretary to the emperor, wrote an account of the campaign (in which he participated) in French, an account which was turned into Latin by Johannes Etrobius and published later in the century. The humanist Juan Ginés de Sepúlveda, who had exhorted the emperor to go on crusade in 1529 and became an imperial chaplain in 1536, wrote a narrative of the campaign, *De bello africo*, in the classical style, although it was not published at the time. The imperial secretary Johannes Secundus (1511-36) was commissioned to write a Latin epic on the subject, but died before he could carry out the task.

Visual images also recorded and spread the knowledge of the campaign. Frescoes in the imperial palace of Granada represented the main events of the campaign. Heemskerck painted the capture of Tunis and the painting was later engraved in order to reach a wider audience. The painter Jan Vermeyen was ordered to accompany the campaign in order to record it as faithfully as possible, making him an early example of the official war artist. The artist Pieter Coecke (1502-50) may also have gone to Tunis for the same reason.

The series of tapestries designed by Vermeyen and representing the campaign has been described, by the art historian Hendrik Horn as 'the perfect embodiment of Charles V's taste in propaganda, and the most important expression in art of his idea of empire'. In this case Latin captions clarify and reinforce the painted messages. For example, Charles is described as gathering his forces at the muster in Barcelona 'with the blessings of heaven (*auspicio divum*)'. At the fall of the fortress La Goleta, 'Caesar comes to the rescue'. Following this, 'The determined Charles (*infestus Carolus*) directs his troops towards Tunis'. The gratitude of the 20,000 Christian captives supposed to have been released by the emperor is also emphasized. The frequency with which all these incidents were represented for the rest of Charles's reign makes a dramatic contrast with the virtual invisibility of the emperor's attack on Algiers in 1541, which ended in inglorious retreat. It reminds us that silence is an important weapon in the armoury of propaganda.

6. The German campaigns

Charles's next victory was against the Duke of Cleves in 1543, which led to the incorporation of Guelderland and Zutphen into what became the seventeen provinces of the Netherlands. Heemskerck represented the defeated Duke on his knees before the emperor, who sits on an improvised throne in the middle of his tent.

Much more important for Charles's self-representation, however, was his campaign against the Schmalkaldic league of the Protestant princes and the victory of Mühlberg, followed by the submission of the rebels. The victory was described in Charles's memoirs as the result of God's assistance and a divine punishment for the 'insolence' of the Landgrave of Hesse and the Protestants in general, who 'had completely lost any sense of shame' (*tinham jà de todo perdida a vergonha*). In public the war, like the Tunis campaign, was presented in triumphalist terms.

During the war, it was the Protestants who produced most of the 153 surviving occasional pieces, mainly songs and newssheets, perhaps because as the rebels they felt a greater need than the supporters of the government to justify their actions. It was Charles, however, who had the last word. Descriptions of the submission of the elector John Frederick of Saxony and the

Landgrave Philip of Hesse were published in 1547, and so was a hymn of triumph, the *Cantilena imperatoria*. Narrative histories of the campaign followed. One of them, by the archdeacon Barnabé de Busto, appointed historian to the emperor in 1546, was never published, but the manuscript is still to be found in the Escorial library. Another was published in 1548, the unofficial or semi-official *Commentari della guerra fatta nella Germania da Carlo Quinto*, written by Giovanni de Godoi, secretary to the prince of Sulmona (a soldier in Charles's service), and printed in Venice. Godoi presents Charles as himself drawing up his squadrons in order and encouraging his troops to fight (*confortando tutti al combattere*). Charles's own account of the battle is worth citing here as a contrast in styles of presentation. The emperor pointed out that a fog prevented the imperial army from seeing the enemy at first, but 'placing everything in the hands of God' (*pondo o emperador tudo nas mãos de Deus*), it pleased Him to lift the fog so that the attack went well.

However, the most important description and glorification of this war is to be found in another 'commentary' by Luis de Avila, *Comentario de la guerra de Alemania 1546 y 1547*, published not long after the end of the campaign not only in the original Spanish (with seven editions by 1552), but also in Italian, French, Flemish, Latin and English. Avila's text is clearly modelled on the *Commentaries* of Julius Caesar. 'Caesar' (as the emperor is described throughout), is shown to display valour and military skill in the field, together with magnanimity and moderation in victory. He is shown exhorting his troops to fight, with an elaborate oration, and exposing himself to enemy fire (he was narrowly missed by a cannon ball). His knowledge of the geography of Germany and his memory of the names of his soldiers (which was to become legendary) are emphasized. Departing from the model of Caesar, Avila described wonders which showed that God was on the emperor's side, notably the signs in the sky on the day of the battle of Mühlberg, the bloody sun boding disaster for Charles's enemies.

On the other hand, the Protestant princes did not come very well out of Avila's version of events. According to the English humanist Roger Ascham, who was in Germany in 1550, Avila was criticized by Albert of Brandenberg for defaming the honour of the princes and was even challenged to a duel, but the emperor would not allow the combat to take place.

The complementary theme of imperial clemency was emphasized in an imperial document issued in May 1548, the Interim of Augsburg, emphasising the need for Christian concord and the manner in which His Imperial Majesty 'took thought in a paternal, troubled and anxious manner (*paternè, sollicitè et anxiè cogitavit*)', as to how to end the conflict, labouring vehemently for a general council and a christian Reformation.

Another influential account of the war may be found in the work by the German Protestant humanist Johann Sleidan (1506-66), *De statu religionis et reipublicae Carolo Quinto Cesare commentarii*, published in Strasbourg in 1555. This work is essentially a history of the German Reformation, describing the links between religion and politics. It is written in a plain style, like the memoirs of Caesar to which Sleidan's title *commentarii*, like Godoi's and Luis de Avila's, makes an obvious reference. The events are related in a cool, detached manner, 'just as they happened' (*prout quaeque res acta fuit*), as the author put it, a detachment truly remarkable given the fact that Sleidan held an official appointment as historian to the Schmalkaldic League (though Luther himself had taught his followers to respect and obey their rulers). Sleidan criticized Avila precisely because his account of the emperor's deeds was not sufficiently impartial.

The best-known contemporary visual images of the campaign against the Protestant princes reinforced Avila's triumphalist message. A medal struck to commemorate the defeat of the Schmalkaldic League showed Charles as Jupiter with a thunderbolt in each hand, and a motto from Virgil's *Aeneid* (VI, 620), 'Heed the warning of justice' (DISCITE IUSTITIAM MONITI). A woodcut by the Italian engraver Enea Vico represented the imperial army crossing the Elbe immediately before the victory. A circular shield made in the 1550s represented the surrender of the elector of Saxony.

Triumphalism is also the keynote of two of the most famous of all the images of the emperor, both of which should probably be linked to this campaign.

Around the year 1549 Leone Leoni made a remarkable life-size statue of Charles in detachable armour, so that he can also be shown naked, like a classical god. The emperor, spear in hand stands over a chained figure. A Latin inscription, 'Fury tamed by the courage of Caesar' (*Caesaris virtuti domitus Furor*) suggests that the chained figure personifies forces of disorder. The inscription may allude to Virgil's praise of Augustus repressing the fury of the crowd in Book 1 of the *Aeneid*. There may also be an allusion to some famous lines in a poem by Petrarch, 'Courage will take arms against fury' (*Virtù contra il furore/Prendera l'arme*), a passage quoted by Machiavelli at the end of his *Prince*.

The image has been interpreted in a number of ways, as Charles defeating the Turk, for example, or as Charles conquering himself. The problem turns on the identification of Fury. This personification is particularly appropriate in a context of rebellion, thus supporting the interpretation of a contemporary Italian cleric, Giovanni Andrea Gilio da Fabriano, who saw the statue as an allegory of the war against the protestant princes.

The most memorable image of Charles, the equestrian portrait by Titian, also represents the victor of Mühlberg, 'riding the same horse' (as the Italian writer Pietro Aretino claimed in a letter to Titian in 1548), 'and wearing the same armour that he had the day he won the battle in Saxony' (*su lo stesso cavallo e con le medesime armi che aveva il dì che vinse la giornata in Saxonia*). The image may also illustrate the description by Luis de Avila of the emperor on horseback at Mühlberg carrying a lance 'almost like a javelin' and wearing the armour made for him by Desiderius Colman of Augsburg.

However, for contemporary viewers the painting is likely to have evoked other associations, some of which may well have been intended by Titian. It presents the emperor as a medieval knight, a hero from a romance of chivalry or the 'knight of Christ' (*miles Christi*), represented in a woodcut by Dürer which would have been well known both to Titian and to contemporary viewers. Charles's lance, or spear, may allude to the lance with which St George slew the dragon, or to the holy lance used at the Crucifixion and preserved (so Charles's contemporaries believed) in the imperial treasury in Vienna. At the same time, the portrait may be regarded a kind of painted equestrian monument in the classical style, given its allusion to the famous equestrian statue of Marcus Aurelius, and also, perhaps, to a medal of the same emperor, the very man who had once been proposed by Guevara as a model for Charles to imitate. In that case the lance or spear may be read as an allusion to the fact that in ancient Rome this weapon was regarded as a symbol of supreme power.

The German campaign was central to the series of twelve engravings of Charles's *Victories* by Maarten van Heemskerck, published in 1556, with inscriptions in Latin, French and Spanish. No fewer than four of the engravings represented episodes in the campaign: the emperor inspecting his troops at Ingolstadt, the surrender of the Elector of Saxony, the submission of the German cities, and the submission of the Landgrave of Hesse, on his knees (like the Duke of Cleves in 1543), before the throne on which Charles sits, with an inscription declaring that the 'previously untamed' Landgrave is 'now more gentle than a lamb' (*ante indomitus/Nunc vel mansuetior agno*). The Elector and the Landgrave were also represented in the first engraving of the series, showing the emperor among his vanquished enemies.

7. The abdication

The imperial play's last act was the staging of Charles's abdication in Brussels. The event was a public one and it was ritualized, despite the problem of the lack of precedent which made the occasion very different from a coronation or funeral. Accounts of the abdication were printed at the time, the Spanish *Renunciación*, for example, published in Valencia in 1556, although these accounts were not numerous. It is largely from the testimonies of ambassadors and other officials that the details of the event are recorded, including homely details such as the emperor entering the hall with a stick, for example, leaning on the Prince of Orange, putting on his spectacles to read his notes, or weeping, like the audience, in the course of his speech.

The public and formal aspects of the ritual also deserve emphasis. The abdication itself was preceded by a ceremony on 22 October in which Charles resigned his Grand Mastership of the Order of the Golden Fleece in favour of his son Philip in the presence of the knights, whom he asked to serve his son faithfully. The abdication itself took place at 4 p. m. on 25 October in the great hall of the palace of Brussels, before an audience of about a thousand people, including Charles's two sisters, his nephews and his niece, the Council of State, the Privy Council, foreign ambassadors and the deputies to the States-General of the seventeen provinces of the Netherlands.

Charles was dressed in black (in 'mourning', according to contemporary observers), and wore the collar of the Golden Fleece. Tapestries representing the Golden Fleece and the Old Testament hero Gideon, also associated with a fleece, were displayed in the hall. The emperor took his seat on a dais, with Philip seated on his right and Maria of Hungary on his left. Philibert of Brussels, a member of the imperial privy council, explained to the assembly the reasons for Charles's abdication. Then the emperor rose and spoke in French from his notes. The speech itself was reminiscent of the emperor's memoirs in its references to the precise number of his many journeys. It also emphasized his poor health and consequent need to lay down the burden of office. Charles then turned to his son, who knelt before him. Raising him up, Charles addressed Philip in Spanish, investing him with office and recommending him to defend the faith and rule his subjects in peace and justice.

On the following day, Charles signed a document transferring power to his son, while the deputies of the States-General swore an oath to obey Philip, who in turn took an oath to observe their laws and maintain their privileges.

As testimony to the way in which the abdication struck contemporaries, we may turn to a detached observer, a Frenchman. Joachim Du Bellay's poem, published in 1558, described Charles as follows: 'He who was the terror of land and sea, weary of his burden, wants to confine his greatness to a cloister and to abandon the world in order to serve God'.

Celui qui fut de la terre et de l'onde
le tonnerre et l'effroy, las de porter le faiz,
veult d'un cloistre borner le grandeur de ses faicts
Et pour servir à Dieu abandonner le monde.

Charles did indeed 'abandon the world' in the sense of retiring to a monastery in Yuste. According to a contemporary Spanish broadside (*pliego suelto*) with the significant title *Relación de la mayor hazaña de Carlo Quinto* (Account of Charles V's greatest exploit), the emperor became an ascetic, sharing the simple food of the monks (in fact he continued to indulge himself in his customary way).

There only remained the last scene of the last act, Charles's death. Dying was a semi-public event for many people at this time, often stage-managed by the clergy, and the emperor's death-bed was no exception. Its most unusual feature was that Charles called for three paintings of Titian, on which to meditate in order; the portrait of his wife Isabel, a painting of Christ's Agony in the Garden, and finally the famous scene of the Last Judgement, known as the Gloria, which represents the emperor in heaven. Charles then received extreme unction and died surrounded by clergy – his confessor, the archbishop of Toledo, and a number of monks.

Assistants

As was noted at the beginning of this essay, Charles's 'self-representation' was in practice a collective enterprise involving considerable numbers of people in different capacities.

Until her death in 1530, Charles's aunt Margaret of Austria may reasonably be regarded as his principal image-manager. She it was, for instance, who appointed Jean Lemaire des Belges and Heinrich Cornelius Agrippa official historians or chroniclers (*chronista* is the term normally used in the documents). Margaret also employed a number of the artists who made well-known images of the emperor (including Meit, Orley, Péril and Vermeyen), some of whom later worked for Charles himself. After Margaret's death, Maria of Hungary played a similar role, although by this time Charles was himself taking more initiatives in this sphere.

Among the many assistants to Charles in the enterprise of self-representation, his ministers and secretaries have an important place, since they wrote many of his letters and speeches as well as taking decisions in his name. Some of the emperor's speeches, for example, were composed by his chancellor Mercurio de Gattinara and others by Pedro Ruiz Mota, the imperial almoner and bishop of Badajoz. Historians have often argued that Gattinara in particular played a decisive role in formulating not only policies but Charles's vision of his imperial role and destiny. Their argument is supported by the fact that the phrase 'universal monarchy', so prominent in the writings of Gattinara, is used less frequently in official documents after the chancellor's death in 1530.

The 'ghost-writing' of the letters and even the speeches of rulers by councillors or secretaries of state was not an unusual practice at this time. Among Charles's secretaries, Jean Lalemand, seigneur de Bouclans, was a leading figure until his disgrace in 1528. So was Francisco de los Cobos, who was in charge of the emperor's correspondence from 1517 onwards, and Nicolas Perrenot de Granvelle, who was secretary for northern Europe from 1530 till his death in 1550. The letters would bear the imperial signature ('Carolus' or 'Yo el Rey'), but underneath one or more secretaries might also sign their names, 'Lalemand', 'Covos', and so on.

The secretaries mentioned so far were something like what we call 'ministers', travelling with the emperor, advising him, or administering a region when he was away from it. Indeed, they needed secretaries of their own. As we have seen, the chancery was the privileged site in this period for the construction of the image of the ruler, and the imperial chancery was staffed by a gifted international team. Secretaries in this stricter sense included Antoine Perrenin, already mentioned for his history of the Tunis campaign, and the Spanish humanist Alfonso de Valdés, whose presentation of Charles's case against Francis I and Clement VII has also been described. Valdés showed the manuscript of his dialogue on the sack of Rome to his colleagues, including Lallemand and Gattinara, and the text was discussed in a session of the imperial council. The councillors Charles de Poupet, seigneur de La Chaulx and Louis de Flandres, seigneur de Praet (d. 1555), were among those who expressed opinions on the subject.

The imperial secretaries also included Guillaume van Male (Maele or Malinaeus, died 1560), a patrician from Bruges. It was to him that Charles dictated his memoirs, in French, in 1550, on a boat on the Rhine in the course of travelling from Cologne to Mainz. It was also van Male who translated them into Latin. He hoped to publish this Latin version, but the emperor did not hand over the manuscript, as if he had some reservations about the publication. Johannes Secundus, an imperial secretary best known today as a Latin poet, had a wider range of duties. He designed medals of the emperor, wrote poems on the coronation at Bologna and the peace of Cambrai, and was commissioned, as we have seen, to write an epic describing the Tunis campaign.

Another important group which participated in the making of the emperor's image were his official historians. It was in the course of the fifteenth century that it became customary for European rulers to pay salaries to men of letters to produce accounts of their deeds for the benefit of posterity. At least eleven historians, seven of whom were Spaniards, were appointed to this position by Charles in the course of the reign with a salary of 80, 000 *maravedis* a year: the Italian humanist Pietro Martire of Anghiera (1521), best known for his history of the discovery of the New World; the Sicilian Bernardo Gentile, a Dominican friar who was appointed in 1523 (to the post which had been left vacant by the death of Antonio Nebrija the year before), and published a Latin poem about Charles in 1526; Antonio de Guevara, court preacher and later bishop (1526); the German humanist Heinrich Cornelius Agrippa, (1529), better known for his interest in the occult, who produced an account of the imperial coronation; the Italian bishop Paolo Giovio (1532); the humanist Juan Ginés de Sepúlveda (1536); Florián de Ocampo, a pupil of the famous humanist Antonio de Nebrija (1539); Alonso de Santa Cruz (c. 1540), who was also the emperor's cosmographer; the theologian Barnabé de Busto (1546); the writer Pedro Mexia (1548) and the philologist Juan Paéz de Castro (1555).

The number of official historians appointed by the emperor was unusually high for the period, comparable only to the appointments made by Charles's grandfather Maximilian. Some of them failed to produce, like Guevara and Ocampo, or wrote texts which were never published, like Busto's account of the Schmalkaldic war, the manuscript of which is in the Escorial library.

On the other hand, accounts of the reign were also produced by writers in the emperor's entourage who did not hold positions as official historians. Curiously enough, the Spanish historian who probably did most to enhance the emperor's image, the courtier Luis de Avila, (whose account of the war against the Protestant princes has already been discussed), was never appointed a *chronista*. Officials who wrote history without being official historians also included the emperor's librarian Guillaume Snouckaert van Schouwenburg (1518-65), who published a biography of Charles in 1559; and Jean Vandenesse, an accountant employed in the imperial household, who wrote a description of Charles's travels. To this group of semi-official texts one might add praise-poems such as the *Triunfo nuptial* (1526) and the *Triunfo real* (1530), by Vasco Díaz Tanco, *La Carolea* (1540), by Jerónimo Sempere, and *Carlo famoso* by the courtier Luis Zapata, even if these works were not officially commissioned.

How many artists worked for the emperor the evidence does not allow us to say. Sculptors included Hans Daucher, who made two statues of Charles in 1522; Jean Mone, who was officially described as Charles's *familiaris*, in other words a member of the emperor's household; the Italian Leone Leoni, who was discovered by cardinal Granvelle and became a member of the imperial household in 1549, the year that *Charles Taming Fury* was commissioned, and his son Pompeo (c. 1533-1608), who designed Charles's tomb

Painters in imperial service included Bernart van Orley, who was already working for Charles in 1516; Christoph Weiditz of Augsburg (c. 1500-59), painter and medallist, who accompanied Charles to Spain in 1529; António de Holanda (c. 1480-1557), a Flemish herald, who painted the emperor's portrait at Toledo in 1529; Christoph Amberger of Augsburg (c. 1505-c. 1563), who painted Charles at the imperial diet in 1532 as well as restoring items in the emperor's collection; Jan Vermeyen, who was in Spain working for Charles in 1534, before accompanying him on the Tunis campaign of 1535 as what would later be known as a `war artist'; Pieter Coecke of Aalst, who styled himself 'imperial painter to Charles V', and may have participated in the Tunis campaign; and Titian, who was introduced to Charles by Federico Gonzaga of Mantua, and was appointed Knight of the Golden Spur and Count Palatine in return for his memorable portraits of the emperor.

An outer circle of artists worked for people who were close to Charles if not for the emperor directly (the evidence is not always clear on the latter point). For example, the Netherlander Conrad Meit, who made a bust of Charles in 1517, worked for Margaret of Austria. At that age it is hardly surprising to discover that the emperor was not in charge of his image. More intriguing is the fact that the artists responsible for the famous images of the coronation cavalcade of 1530 were in the service of Margaret, not her nephew: Robert Péril of Antwerp and Nicolaus Hogenberg (c. 1500-39) of Munich.

Other members of the family also employed artists who made images of Charles. Jacob Seisenegger, who painted the famous full-length portrait of Charles in 1532, was employed as court painter to Charles's brother Ferdinand. Giulio Clovio (1498-1578), who illustrated the emperor's victories, worked for Maria of Hungary, who was also the patron of Leone Leoni, Jan Vermeyen and (like Margaret of Austria) Bernard van Orley. Leone also made a bust of Charles for cardinal Granvelle. The fact that the same artists were employed directly by the emperor and also by members of his entourage makes it virtually impossible to decide which commissions were 'official', The distinction between the official and unofficial spheres was in any case much less sharp at this time than it would become in later centuries.

One of the most interesting questions to ask about these assistants – and unfortunately, one of the most difficult to answer – is the extent to which they had their own agenda. Gattinara, for example, had his own vision of the empire, which he did his best to instil into his young master. Alfonso de Valdés, like his master Erasmus and his friend the Valencian humanist Juan Luis Vives, wanted Charles to hold a general council in order to reform the church.

The fact that these assistants had views of their own rather than following any clear imperial directive makes it even more difficult to draw any firm line between official and unofficial presentations of the emperor. One shades into the other. One tapestry of the victory at Pavia, for example, was commissioned by Charles himself, but another was made by order of the States-General of the Netherlands for presentation to the emperor. Despite the difference in patronage, it is difficult to guess which tapestry is which. The same point might be made about medals, comparing the medal of 1521 presented to the emperor by the city of Nuremberg with the ones by artists in imperial service.

Again, one might take the case of entries into cities. It is obviously important to distinguish between cities which were subject to the emperor (like Bruges, Zaragoza, and Naples), and cities which were not (Paris, for example, or Rome). In the official account of Charles's Paris entry of 1540, for instance, there is a resounding silence on the subject of Charles's victories. In the case of the coronation at Bologna, which was organized in part by imperial and in part by papal officials, there is evidence of a struggle for dominance within the rituals themselves. Within the church, where the space was under papal control, Charles was given a throne lower than that of the pope, but in the procession through the streets, the emperor's soldiers clearly outnumbered the pope's men.

Even in the case of Bruges in 1515, an entry into a city under imperial rule, the civic programme took the form of a petition rather than a panegyric. The main theme selected on that occasion for display in the eleven pageants for which the local chamber of rhetoric wrote the programme was that of the history of the city, especially its recent decline. The eighth pageant, for example, represented the golden age of the city, with Bruges personified by a maiden sitting on a golden throne accompanied by the Burgundian princes Philip the Good and Charles the

Bold and a woman personifying trade (*Marchandise*). The ninth pageant, by contrast, showed the more recent silver age with Bruges seated on a silver throne and *Marchandise* preparing to leave. The final pageant represented a wheel of fortune, at the bottom of which sat a female figure once again personifying the city itself. An inscription reinforced the message: 'sir, do not cease helping your poor subjects' (*sire ne retire la main de layde de tes povres subiectz*). This was not propaganda for Charles so much as propaganda addressed to Charles on behalf of the city.

A writer who does not fit easily into either the 'official' or the 'unofficial' categories is that of Pietro Aretino, who was pensioned by the emperor but was very much his own man. Aretino wrote for the market, represented by the printers of Venice, precisely in order to keep his independence, though he was far from averse to gifts from princes, who may well have decided to pay him for fear of what he might write about them if they did not. Sometimes he flattered the emperor, sometimes he advised him, as in the case of a letter of 1527 about the sack of Rome, in which the writer asked Charles to free the pope.

Another marginal example is that of the poet Ludovico Ariosto. In the fifteenth canto of his epic *Orlando Furioso*, Ariosto introduced a vision of the future (as Virgil had done in the *Aeneid*), in which Andronica sees the victorious captains of Charles V, 'the wisest and the most just emperor that there had been or ever would be after Augustus (*il più saggio imperatore e giusto/che sia stato o sarà mai dopo Augusto*)'. According to this vision, Astraea, goddess of justice, will return to earth and Charles will rule the world, because God wishes it; 'and he wants there to be only one flock and one shepherd under this emperor (*e vuol che sotto a questo imperatore/solo un ovile sia, solo un pastore*)'. This passage, lacking in the first edition of the poem, was inserted after 1529, when relations were improving between the emperor and the poet's prince, Alfonso d'Este, Duke of Ferrara. It might therefore be regarded as a semi-official presentation.

So might the statue of Charles which was displayed at the festival in Florence in 1539 to celebrate the wedding of Cosimo de'Medici, Duke of Tuscany, with Eleanora of Toledo. Like Alfonso d'Este, Cosimo was technically an independent ruler, but as a new prince he was in particular need of support and so he gravitated to the orbit of the emperor. Indeed, it was at Charles's suggestion that Cosimo married Eleanora, one of the daughters of Pedro de Toledo, the emperor's viceroy in Naples.

On the other hand, the classicizing representation of the making of peace between Charles and Francis in the form of the closing of the doors of the Temple of Peace, painted by the Florentine artist Francesco Salviati (1510-63), was designed to glorify the pope who had brokered the agreement, Paul III Farnese, and decorated his family palace. The later paintings of Charles by Taddeo Zuccaro (1529-66) made for the 'room of the Farnese deeds' in the family's country house at Caprarola near Viterbo had a similar purpose.

The emperor's role

To what extent Charles himself was interested in the visual arts is a matter of controversy between scholars, who range from describing him as 'an avid patron of the arts', as Marie Tanner does, to stressing his 'lack of interest', like Fernando Checa. It may be possible to resolve this conflict by making distinctions between kinds of image and periods in the emperor's life. Charles was always interested in having his victories recorded, but until about 1530 he left other commissions to his aunt and his sister. After his meeting with Titian in 1529, however, the emperor's interest in art and artists seems to have developed.

From the late 1520s, Charles himself seems to have taken an increasing interest in the way in which he was represented, and he was sometimes critical of the results. For example, he did not approve of the Valdés dialogue on the Sack of Rome 'because', as a contemporary commented, 'he is much devoted to images (*porque es muy devoto de imágines*). However, the text was defended by his privy councillors the seigneurs de Lachaux and Praet. Valdés also wrote a Latin account of the abortive duel between the two kings which Charles wanted to look at, although the emperor was not sure of the wisdom of printing it, as Valdés explained in a letter to the Polish humanist Johannes Dantiscus in January 1529.

In the 1530s, the emperor showed even more interest in the way in which he was portrayed, witness his relations with Titian and other painters. He appreciated the work of Seisenegger, Vermeyen and António de Holanda, telling the latter's son that António had portrayed him better at Toledo than Titian at Bologna. His Burgundian tastes are revealed in his interest in ritual and in his interest in translating Olivier de la Marche's allegorical romance of chivalry *Le Chevalier délibéré*. In the 1540s, the emperor's reform of Spanish court ritual on the model of the court of Burgundy reveals his personal concern with the setting in which he was displayed.

Charles's personal concern for his future place in history is also revealed by his appointment of chroniclers, his drafting of his many political testaments (reminiscent of the advice of the emperor Marcus Aurelius to his son as recounted by Guevara), and finally by his decision to dictate his memoirs, which he revised in Augsburg and again in retirement at Yuste. Comparisons with Caesar's *Commentaries* were inevitable and they were probably intentional, since one of the few books Charles is known to have had with him at Yuste was an Italian translation of Caesar.

In the pages of Sepúlveda's history (especially Book 30, chapter 31), Charles appears as a plain, honest man, 'Not cunning, not deceitful, but a lover of the simple truth' (*Non astutus, non fallax, sed simplicis veritatis amator*). The historian reports a conversation in which he offered to show the emperor what he had written, while Charles waved him away. 'Let other people read this when I am dead' (*Legent alii, cum ipse a vita discessero*). However, there is evidence to suggest that this modesty was itself a fabrication, part of the official image. When he was living in retirement at Yuste, Charles told his daughter Juana to ensure the publication of the work of both Sepúlveda and Ocampo.

Even more revealing is Charles's reaction to the work of Paolo Giovio, the humanist bishop who wrote a history of his own time based to a large extent on interviews with participants, from rulers and generals down to galley-slaves. The Milanese physician Girolamo Cardano recorded the story of Charles's angry reaction to Giovio's account of the battle of Pavia: 'Giovio has not described my victory but that of the King of France'. This story may be apocryphal. The emperor's personal interest in Giovio's account of the Tunis campaign, on the other hand, is well documented.

In 1550, Giovio sent to the imperial court a draft of book 34 of his 'history of his own time' (*Historia sui temporis*), the part dealing with the expedition to Tunis. He included a covering letter to cardinal Granvelle, saying that he had learned of the emperor's personal interest in the view that posterity would have of him. The reply to Giovio was drafted by Don Luis de Avila and translated into Latin by Guillaume van Male. In other words, the response came from two of the people most closely involved with the presentation of the image of the emperor.

The comments which he made on the draft version show that Avila was not altogether happy with Giovio's account of the campaign. For example, Don Luis recommended placing more emphasis on Charles's role at the battle of Goletta, on his exposure to enemy fire, for example, his speech to his soldiers and his personal decision to launch an attack. Giovio promised to revise his story, but in practice his only emendation was to insert the bland phrase 'with the encouragement of the emperor' (*cohortante Cesare*). As the Florentine ambassador reported back to his master Grand Duke Cosimo de' Medici, Charles 'is so covetous of glory that he has regarded this history with an extremely jaundiced eye; for it seems to him that Giovio has detracted from his figure or from the truth'.

The publics

Little is known so far, for lack of serious research on the subject, about the various publics to whom Charles was presented, the different regions and social groups, and their different responses to the official image. What follows is therefore no more than a provisional reconnaissance of a virtually unexplored territory.

Some of the surviving images of the emperor were privately commissioned for the personal use of individuals. They include a enamel hat jewel with the portrait of Charles, a magnificent stone mantelpiece in a private house in Bruges representing Charles and his grandparents, and of course many portraits. Woodcuts, engravings and etchings were relatively cheap and included portraits of the emperor by Daniel Hopfer (c. 1517), Hans Baldung (1519), Barthel Beham (1531), Frans Huys, Jan Vermeyen, and Enea Vico (1550). To this group of images should be added many book illustrations and also Maarten van Heemskerk's series of Charles's victories (1555-6), engraved by Dirck Coornhert. The victories were published by Hieronymus Cock of Antwerp with captions in Flemish (composed by Coornhert) and also, to reach an international public, in Latin (composed by the Flemish humanist Hadrianus Junius).

However, the evidence for the diffusion of the visual image of Charles cannot be confined to those artefacts which happen to have survived to this day. It needs to be supplemented from inventories post mortem, listing the worldly goods of the deceased. By this means it is possible to learn, for instance, that two Calvinists from Antwerp, Jan van der Noot and Cornelis Rosseau, despite their opposition to Charles's religious policies, both owned paintings of the victories of the emperor. Such examples are no more than the tip of an enormous iceberg.

The literary image of the emperor was also widespread. In Spain, for example, he was the hero of a number of ballads (*romances*), which were printed on single sheets (*pliegos sueltos*) in order to be sold in the street. The figure of the emperor also recurs in the German and Flemish ballads of this time, some of them making comments in his favour and some against, while yet others are open-minded or indecisive. 'Kaiser Karl' is generally presented as 'well-born' (*hochgeborn*), 'pious' (*fromme*), and 'brave' (*coragieus*), 'an honourable man' (*ein ehrlich Mann*) and a man supported by God. 'Through Charles, the Lord God gives us his sign' (*Durch Carolum gibt uns Gott der Herr sein Segen*). These ballads were generally occasioned by particular events and may be regarded as the sixteenth-century equivalent of newspapers (it was only in the early seventeenth century that regular news-sheets began to be produced).

Stories about the emperor which spread by word of mouth are occasionally documented in his lifetime. For example, in a chronicle written in the year 1527 or thereabouts, not for publication but for recitation or circulation in manuscript, the courtier-jester Don Francesillo de Zúñiga (c. 1480-1532) recorded the story of the peasant in Calatayud who told Charles to close his mouth because the flies of the kingdom were insolent (*Nuestro Señor, cerrad la boca; moscas deste reino son traviesas*).

Again, the story of a German soldier who shot at the emperor by mistake at Tunis because he took him for a Spaniard was told by Sepúlveda (Book 11). The story of the wagoner at Speyer was recorded in the memoirs of Bartholomeus Sastrow, who probably heard it in the 1540s. Apparently the wagoner did not recognise the man riding in the vehicle jostling him, struck the emperor with his whip and called him 'you scum of a Spaniard'. As a punishment, Charles only ordered the man's nose to be cut off, an act of mercy for which the victim apparently 'sang the praises of the emperor'.

A number of the emperor's sayings, whether genuine or apocryphal, were also recorded in his lifetime. Zuñiga's burlesque chronicle, quoted above, tells various stories of the emperor's insults to his courtiers, stories which follow the same pattern. To the Count of Aranda, for example, Charles is supposed to have said, 'Count, you look like a bitch which is sitting down cracking bones' (*Conde, pareceis cachorra asentada, que se està royendo huesos*). Charles's verdict on Sir Thomas More at least sounds more authentic. Writing a biography of Sir Thomas in the 1550s, his son-in-law William Roper (1496-1578) recorded the emperor's comment on More's execution twenty years before, a comment which had been passed on to him by the English diplomat Sir Thomas Elyot: 'We would rather have lost the best city of our dominions than have lost such a worthy councillor'.

Needless to say, it cannot be assumed that the public, or better, the various publics of his time, always viewed Charles in the way that he and his advisers desired. Some discrepancies between the imperial image and everyday reality were already obvious enough. The evidence of his illegitimate children, notably Margaret of Parma and Don John of Austria, demonstrated that Charles was not as chaste as he was reported to be. Again, the Algiers campaign did not do much to support the triumphalist image of an ever-victorious emperor.

Less favourable images of the emperor must not be forgotten either. The detachment of the Venetian ambassadors and the cool assessments of Charles's strengths and weaknesses in their reports, from Francesco Corner in 1521 to Federico Badoer in 1557, have already been mentioned. It is from them that we have inherited the famous image of the stuttering emperor. Hostile views of Charles were also in circulation. One of them is recorded in passing by a later Spanish historian, Sandoval (below, 98), when describing Charles's visit to Genoa. According to Sandoval, the Genoese were relieved to discover that the emperor was not a Gothic barbarian. They had apparently expected another Totila, 'restless, cruel, a lover of wars, rough, a man with whom it was impossible to negotiate (*inquieto, cruel, amigo de guerras, aspero, intratable*).

Needless to say, the French helped spread unfavourable images of this kind. Francis I, like Charles, published an apologia at the time of the League of Cognac, presenting his version of events. In his comic romance *Gargantua* (1534), François Rabelais gave King Picrochole, the enemy of his giant-hero Gargantua, some of the traits of the emperor, referring for example to a device of `two columns more magnificent than those of Hercules' (*deux colonnes plus magnificques que celles de Hercules*) (chapter 33).

The English humanist Roger Ascham's *Report on the Affairs of Germany*, which was published in 1552, together with his franker private letters, which remained unpublished until the eighteenth century presented an image of the emperor as a badly-dressed glutton, who 'drank the best that ever I saw; he had his head in the glass five times as long as any of us, and never drank less than a good quart at once of Rhenish wine'. Ascham also described the emperor as a failure as a politician, 'blinded with the over-good opinion of his own wisdom', despising 'all advice of others', and to make matters worse, manipulated by the pope (it should be remembered that Ascham was a zealous Protestant). The author also notes Charles's ingratitude and his failure to keep faith with the Ottoman sultan.

It is unlikely that favourable and unfavourable images of the emperor were transmitted by completely separate channels to reach quite different publics. On some occasions at least, individuals must have been confronted with rival and even contradictory images of Charles, and forced to make up their own minds about what to believe.

Charles in comparative perspective

To place the self-presentation of Charles V in historical perspective, it may be useful to offer some comparisons between his official image and that of some of his contemporaries and rivals. The Ottoman Sultan Suleiman the Magnificent, for instance, was one of the few rulers in the world whose power was comparable to that of Charles. Muslim traditions denied him the opportunity of displaying his portrait in public in the way that Charles did (or indeed Suleiman's predecessor Mehmed II). Nor did the sultan employ the medium of print, the use of which was confined in the Ottoman Empire at this time to Jewish and Christian minorities. All the same, Suleiman 'The Lawgiver' (*Kanuni*), as he was described at the time in his own culture, appears to have understood very well the importance of self-presentation. His clothes, jewels and weapons all enhanced his appearance. His travels in Anatolia made his face well known to his subjects, like his weekly ride to the mosque in Istanbul and the more formal rituals of his annual departure on campaign and his return. Suleiman established the position of official historian (*sehnameci*). A biography of the sultan produced in his lifetime, the *Sulayman-name*, celebrated him as a world-conqueror in a manner parallel to the presentation of Charles V. Narratives of specific campaigns were also produced, much like the accounts of Charles at Tunis or Mühlberg. The sultan was, incidentally, well aware of Charles's image. Suleiman's procession outside the besieged city Vienna emulated that of Charles at Bologna, and it made similar imperial claims.

Charles's great rival Francis I was also concerned with his public image. The French king's grand building projects at the Louvre, Fontainebleau, Chambord and elsewhere were designed at least in part to present him as a liberal and magnificent patron of the arts, a point which is sometimes emphasised in the decorations themselves, notably those in the Ulysses Gallery at Fontainebleau. Unlike Charles, Francis also took pains to present himself as a ruler who was interested in literature and learning. He ordered the collection of Greek manuscripts for the royal library, for example, he founded the Collège Royal (now the Collège de France), and he rewarded poets. In these ways the king contributed to the myth that he was primarily responsible for the 'revival of letters' in France, a myth which was already current a few years after his death. On the other hand, Francis commissioned fewer portraits of himself and fewer medals representing the events of his reign than the emperor did, and he did not attempt to emulate Charles's heavy investment in official history

These comparisons suggest that a general concern with self-presentation was not unusual among sixteenth-century rulers, but also that Charles, or his close advisers, were unusually concerned with the details of his public image. Why should this have been the case? The fact that the medium of print was now available to rulers helps to account for their increasing interest in their images, but it does nothing to account for the contrasts between Charles and Francis. Perhaps a political explanation is in order. The new stress on the glorious image of the emperor may have been a response to what has been called the 'crisis of imperial power' in the 1520s, when Charles's authority was challenged by rebels both in Spanish cities (the *comuneros*) and the German countryside (the so-called 'Peasant War' of 1525). It might even be suggested that the increasing emphasis on his triumphalist image at the end of Charles's reign was a kind of compensation in the realm of the imagined for the loss of power which the *cuius regio eius religio* settlement made all too apparent.

More than a hundred years later, Louis XIV was even more concerned with his image than Francis or Charles had been. More than three hundred medals were struck to commemorate the major events of his reign. The officially-commissioned painted portraits of Louis run into hundreds, and the engraved portraits total about seven hundred altogether. Statues of Louis were on display in the public squares of Paris and a number of provincial cities, a practice which was virtually unheard-of in the time of Charles (his protégé Grand Duke Cosimo de' Medici of Tuscany was one of the pioneers of the new genre, commissioning an equestrian statue of himself which was erected on Piazza della Signoria in Florence).

An even more important difference between Charles and Louis concerns what might be called the organisation of their image. One of the king's leading ministers, Jean-Baptiste Colbert, spent a good deal of time planning the presentation of Louis after soliciting the advice of men of letters and artists. In the course of the reign, unofficial consultations were replaced by a permanent committee, the so-called `little academy', which examined and criticised projects for the presentation of the king as well as devising the inscriptions for medals.

Compared to that of Louis, the image of Charles V was

fabricated in a much less organized fashion. There were fewer official commissions and a greater reliance on freelance writers in hope of rewards. The emperor had no *petite académie* and it was only on special occasions, like the crisis following the release of Francis I from captivity, that the imperial council discussed how to present Charles in public. Charles, unlike Louis, appears not to have avoided being viewed by foreign diplomats, such as Ascham and the Venetians, when he was off the public stage.

Another major difference which emerges from the comparison with Louis XIV is Charles V's lack of a ritual centre. He had no Versailles: his itinerant life did not allow it. His successors on the Spanish throne, beginning with his son Philip, had two centres, a sacred centre in El Escorial and a centre of secular ritual in the palace at Madrid, but on the other hand they did not have Charles's responsibilities as Holy Roman Emperor.

Charles's widespread international empire posed acute problems of co-ordination, which his travels could alleviate but not solve altogether. The King of England or France could make use of a single official printer in London or Paris, as Francis employed Robert Estienne to publish his letters defending himself against the accusations of the emperor. Charles on the other hand, had to rely for the publication of his speeches or accounts of battles or ceremonies on a diaspora of printers in Alcalá (Miguel de Eguía), Antwerp (Johannes Graphaeus, Martin de Keyser, J. Steelsius and others), Mainz (Johannes Schoeffer), Nuremberg (Johannes Petri), Rome (Antonio Blado, Jacobus Mazochius), and elsewhere. It is far from clear whether these printers, a few of whom regularly published texts about Charles, were subsidised by the government, whether they were officially encouraged, or whether they were simply printing what they thought would sell. Only around 1527 is there any sign of a co-ordinated international campaign to present imperial policies in a particular light.

All the same, his appointment of official historians and his reaction to Giovio's history suggests that the emperor, like Louis XIV, was keenly concerned with influencing the views of posterity. To discover whether or not he was successful in this respect, we shall need to turn to the posthumous images of the emperor.

Re-presenting Charles V, 1558-2000

Although every item in the long list of books and articles by historians devoted to Charles since his death would be relevant to this chapter, what follows is not in essence a historiographical essay, still less a bibliographical one. It is a survey of the changing image of the emperor, among ordinary people as well as intellectuals, among artists and creative writers as well as among historians. Indeed, it is a sketch for a posthumous biography, of the kind produced by the German scholar Friedrich Gundolf on the history of Caesar's reputation (Caesar, Geschichte seines Ruhms, 1924), and by the Dutch historian Pieter Geyl (1887-1966) in his `Napoleon for and Against' (Napoleon. Voor en tegen in de Franse geschiedschrijving, 1946).

Noting what he called `the endless variety of interpretations' of Napoleon, and admitting that history was `an argument without end' which could reach `no unchallengeable conclusions' about such a man, Geyl opted to emphasise the relation between the changing image of Napoleon and `French political and cultural life', showing how the attitudes of scholars to the Church, the Second Empire or the Third Republic shaped their interpretations of the past. Charles V can be studied in the same way. Indeed, as Geyl pointed out, Napoleon himself once cited Charles as a precedent. When he had Pope Pius VII arrested in 1809, the emperor remarked in a letter to Murat that `Charles V kept Clement VII in prison for a long period'.

Given the enormous amount of material dealing with the emperor's life and policies which has been produced over the centuries, it will be necessary in this brief essay to be rigorously selective. All the same, an attempt will be made to follow the model of Geyl and the equally famous advice of the English scholar E. H. Carr (1892-1982), `Before you study history, study the historian', and so to place the biographies of Charles, like his painted images, in their social, cultural and political contexts.

Already widely diffused in his lifetime, the image of the emperor spread still more widely after his death. By 1580, for example, a portrait of Charles was to be seen in Peking. In Istanbul in 1675, the French traveller Jean Baptiste Tavernier saw on display in the sultan's palace at Topkapi a tapestry of Charles enthroned. The Scottish historian William Robertson's study of Charles, published in Arabic in 1842, was, together with books on Napoleon and Peter the Great, one of the first translations from western languages made in the Middle East. The juxtaposition of these three rulers suggests that Charles too had become a symbol of modernity or at least of the will to modernise. In Europe, on the other hand, Charles was variously viewed as a near-saint, as an exemplar of reason of state, as a national hero, and finally as a symbol of European unity.

The Cult of Charles in the Habsburg lands

Philip II, a devoted son, helped shape the first posthumous image of his father by the funeral and memorial services which he arranged, described not long after the event in publications such as *Les obsèques de l'empereur Charles* (1559). The funeral itself took place in Yuste, but it was overshadowed by the re-enactments which were organized in a number of cities, including Toledo, Tarragona, Seville, Valladolid, Lisbon, Rome, Naples, Augsburg, Vienna, in the New World and, most notably, in Brussels.

For example, according to the historian Giorgio Vasari, for the Requiem Mass for Charles celebrated in Rome in 1559, the church of San Giacomo degli Spagnuoli was decorated with a series of thirteen paintings by Taddeo Zuccaro representing imperial victories. In Brussels, the emperor's catafalque in the cathedral displayed his insignia, his four crowns, his sword of state, sceptre and orb, and his collar of the Order of the Golden Fleece. The funeral procession in Brussels, organised according to Burgundian tradition, was a long one and included a helmet made for the occasion banners, standards, and the caparisons of horses all emblazoned with eagles, globes, and Charles's coat of arms. Most magnificent of all was the life-size model `ship of state' which was taken in procession and is said to have cost 75,000 ducats to construct.

The model was a materialization of a traditional political analogy between the ruler and the pilot of a ship, and it also offered a summary of the emperor's virtues and his deeds. Inscriptions on the ship referred to the 'incorporation' (a euphemism for 'conquest') of Guelderland (GUELDRIA RECEPTA), to peace in the Mediterranean (MARE PACATO), to the defeat of the Suleiman at Vienna (SOLYMANO PROFLIGATO), to the capture of Tunis (TUNETO CAPTO), and to the discovery of the New World (ORBE NOVO INVENTO). The emperor's epitaph called Charles the conqueror of France, Africa and Saxony, and the perpetual defender of the Christian commonwealth against the Turks.

Those who had been unable to see any of the funeral rituals and displays for themselves were soon able to read about them. Elaborate engravings of the imperial funeral procession were published by the famous printer Christophe Plantin in Antwerp in 1559, together with explanatory texts in French, German, Spanish, and Italian. The engravings were the work of Jan and Lucas van Doetechum, following sketches by Hieronymus Cock. The engravings had been commissioned by Philip II's herald, Pierre de Vernois, who was in turn reimbursed by Margaret of Parma. In other words, the work was an official publication which was expected to have a wide European appeal.

A number of orations delivered in various places on the occasion of Charles's death were also published at the time, including the *Oratio funebris pro Carolo Quinto*, for instance, by the German jurist Georg Eder (1523-87); the oration delivered at Leuven in the name of the university by the humanist Cornelis Wouters or Valerius (1517-92), which compared the emperor with Charlemagne, Caesar, Alexander and Pompey; and the *Oratio in funere Caroli Quinti* by the Italian rhetorician Francesco Robortello (1516-67), delivered at the Spanish college in Bologna.

A few years later, in 1570, came the publication of the *Túmulo imperial* by Juan Cristóbal Calvete de Estrella (d. 1593), the emperor's former confessor, while in 1573 the corpse of Charles was transferred from Yuste to the Escorial. In 1598, the great funeral monument to Charles designed by Pompeo Leoni (c. 1533-1608), the son of Leone Leoni, was at last ready to be erected in the chapel of the Escorial. The gilded bronze statues of the emperor, his wife, his daughter and his two sisters were placed on one side of the high altar, more or less in conformity to the detailed instructions in Charles's will, which referred to 'a sculpture of the Empress and myself, kneeling, with our heads uncovered and feet bare'.

Copies of Charles's political testaments, with titles such as *Avisos o instrucción del emperador al principe su hijo*, began to circulate in manuscript at this time, presumably with the approval of Philip himself or someone close to him – after all, the documents were confidential, and the king took a close personal interest in his state papers.

Philip's other contribution to the reputation of Charles was the harsh way he dealt or let his representative the duke of Alba deal with the revolt of the Netherlands in the 1570s, thus ensuring that the Netherlanders would look back to the reign of Charles as a golden age. Some of the pamphleteers defending the Revolt of the Netherlands evoked the glorious days of Charles V, presenting him as a ruler who granted privileges generously and respected them when granted – conveniently forgetting the emperor's notorious punishment of Ghent in 1540. The pamphleteers were of course following the classic strategy of criticizing a ruler by contrasting him with a predecessor.

In similar fashion, in the New World, the Franciscan friar Gerónimo de Mendieta (1525-1604), author of the *Historia eclesiástica indiana*, saw the reign of 'The most pious emperor

Charles V, of immortal memory (*El piadosísimo Emperador Carlos V, de inmortal memoria*) as a golden age, that of the revival of the primitive church in the Americas by the friars, as opposed to the silver age of Philip II in which he wrote, the age of the bishops.

The death of Charles was followed by a stream of biographies of the emperor, beginning with the panegyric by Guillaume Snouckaert van Schouwenburg, *Carolus Quintus*, published in Ghent in 1559, which virtually treated the emperor as a saint (as we have seen, the term *sanctitas* was used on the titlepage). When the emperor's body was discovered in 1573, at the time of its move to El Escorial, to have been preserved uncorrupted, Charles's sanctity became clearly apparent, at least to some observers.

In Italy, from the end of the 1550s, a number of professional writers, the so-called *poligrafi*, based in Venice, one of the leading printing centres of the time, produced rival biographies. Among the first were the *Vita di Carlo V* (1558) by the Spanish nobleman Alfonso de Ulloa (1529-c. 1580), published by the Venetian firm of Valgrisi, the *Vita di Carlo V* (1561) by the prolific Ludovico Dolce (1510-68) from the press of the leading Venetian publisher of the time, Giolito, and the *Simolacro di Carlo V* (1567) by Francesco Sansovino. The poet Bernardo Tasso (father of the more famous poet Torquato) also began a life of the emperor. Outside Italy there was Juan Ochoa's *La Carolea* (1585). The title may lead the reader to expect an epic poem, but the text is in fact a dry prose narrative enlivened only by a few prodigies (like the eagle which accompanied the imperial army at Mühlberg) or reports of the sayings of the emperor.

The most successful of these texts, at least from a publishing point of view, was Ulloa's biography, which had reached its seventh edition by 1606, while a Flemish translation followed in 1610. More than seven hundred pages long, and a history of the reign, or even, as the author remarked, of the history of the world during Charles's reign rather than a biography in the strict sense, Ulloa's book presented Charles according to the conventional wisdom of the panegryrists. His protagonist was portrayed as an exemplar of prudence, justice, fortitude, temperance, clemency and liberality. Above all, attention was drawn to the constancy shown by the emperor at times of both good and bad fortune. To bring his portrait to life, Ulloa included the usual details – Charles's interest in clocks, his skill as a rider, his excellent memory (including a memory for individual soldiers), his aquiline nose, (a sign of the royal quality of magnanimity), the religious significance of his retirement to enjoy 'the contemplative life', and his good, indeed his exemplary death (*una morte esemplarissima*).

The poets too commemorated Charles. His exploits were celebrated in *La Carolea* (1560), by the Spanish poet Jerónimo Sempere (fl. 1540-60), and in *Carlos Famoso* (1566) by Luis Zapata (1526-95). Both poems were written in the style of Ariosto, as their first lines suggest. Sempere declares that he will sing of the French, Turks, Moors, Germans and American Indians vanquished by Charles:

Franceses, Turcos, Moros y Germanos

Y gentes de las Indias muy estrañas
Vencidas por el Cesar de Romanos
Invicto y claro Rey de las Españas
Yo canto ...

while Zapata sings of the deeds, enterprises, exploits, courage and power of the emperor:

Los hechos, las empresas, las hazañas
El valor y el poder de Carlo canto ...

Charles himself is described as 'heroic', 'triumphant', 'brave', 'generous', 'pious', and above all 'humane' (*humano*), although he is not shown as doing very much except travelling, being shipwrecked, talking to Henry VIII, receiving a crown and so on. His figure gains in stature, however, by being located in an epic landscape.

Sempere, for example, despite the fact that his poem broke off before it reached the Tunis campaign, stressed the importance of the struggle with the sultan, 'the hungry dragon of Turkey', as he called him (*el hambriento/Dragon de la Turquía*). In the style of the traditional Spanish ballad, the author even showed Suleiman writing a letter to Charles to challenge him to battle. As for Zapata, he described the rebellion of the Spanish *comuneros* in the classicizing epic language of a combat with 'a monstrous beast with many heads' (*una monstruosa bestia de muchas cabezas*).

In the epic by Alonso de Ercilla, *La Araucana* (1569-90), the story of the Spanish conquest of what is now Chile, an epic which, unlike its competitors, is still reprinted today, there were no fewer than fifteen references to Charles, 'el gran Carlos', 'Carlos Quinto Máximo glorioso', 'el gran Emperador, invicto Carlo', and so on.

The Benedictine monk Prudencio de Sandoval (c. 1551-1621), who was appointed chronicler to Philip III in 1599 and later became bishop of Pamplona, was the author of one of what is still one of the best-known accounts of the emperor's life, the *Vida de Carlos V*. The book is full of original documents, including the emperor's letters and the political testaments of 1548 and 1554, and for this reason it continues to be useful to historians. However, the *Vida* is not a detached account, far from it, but a celebration of the 'heroic grandeur' of the emperor's deeds. Charles's genealogy is traced back to Adam via Noah, Osiris and Hercules, while the work of Giovio is the object of repeated criticisms on the grounds that its author had minimized the achievements of the emperor.

As in the case of Snouckaert's panegyric, great emphasis was placed in Sandoval's history on Charles's piety, his devotion to Our Lady of Montserrat, for instance, his exemplary life and religious practices at Yuste, and so on. The author even prints a prayer which the emperor was accustomed to recite every night before he went to sleep. The book was well received in Spain. First published in 1604-6, it went through five editions in the course of the century, as well as being translated into English.

In Sandoval's history, despite the use of original documents, the mythification of the emperor is apparent, at least in places. It is taken still further in a book apparently intended for a wider audience, the *Epitome de la vida y hechos del invicto emperador Carlos Quinto*, by the Spanish nobleman Juan Antonio de Vera y Figueroa, conde de la Roca, a book which had reached its seventh edition by 1654. Anecdotes about the emperor's childhood, his early interest in war, for example, drawing up his pages in squadrons, are presented as 'signs' of his future career. Astrologers and comets reinforce the message that the child will have a great future. In short Roca offers an up-to-date version of the old myth of the childhood of the hero. The end of the emperor's career is presented in similar fashion. Abdication and retirement are described as the last 'exploits' of the monarch (as in the sixteenth-century *pliego suelto* cited above, or the play by Encisco mentioned below), and the book ends with a description of Charles's virtues, including chastity and temperance in eating, 'closer to a philosopher than to a king' (despite the fact that Charles's mistresses and his gluttony were well known in his own day). The wise, worthy, courageous, catholic and other notable sayings of the emperor are also reported and duly emphasised by marginal notes and appropriate entries in the index.

In the Holy Roman Empire too Charles was remembered with respect in the seventeenth century. For example, a teacher in a school in Breslau in 1638, Christophorus Colerus, gave an oration 'On the abilities and fortune (*virtute et fortuna*) of the emperor Charles V', in which he presented Charles as 'led by virtue' and `with fortune as a companion'. In Cologne, a text by the Jesuit Jacobus Masenius, *Anima historiae huius temporis in invicto Caroli V et Ferdinandi I repraesentata* (1672) presented Charles as a moral paragon, the incarnation of piety, humanity and patience, and even praised him for his communicative skills (*facundia dicendi*), a remarkable compliment to an emperor known to have spoken little and with difficulty which is on a par with La Roca's praise of his temperance at the dinner-table.

In the southern Netherlands, a late seventeenth-century text, published in Brussels in both Flemish and French (*De heerlycke ende vrolycke daeden van keyser Carel den V; Les actions heroiques et plaisantes de l'empereur Charles V),* presented him as a model for the rulers of the age, 'le plus beau modèle sur lequel vous puissiez vous former', as the introduction puts it, and 'le plus digne héros que vous puissiez imiter'.

In this text the imperial achievements are summed up in a series of gargantuan statistics – forty victories, eight hundred cities, a hundred thousand castles and so on: (*il a remporté quarante victoires fameuses, conquis huit cents villes, gaigné autant de vaisseaux, et ajouté à ses conquêtes cent mille chateaux*). All the same, what Charles really wanted, so we learn, was 'the quiet of the empire' (*le repos de l'empire*) its conservation rather than its expansion. His 'extraordinary' virtue was revealed by `His moderation in his victories, the clemency he showed to the vanquished and his friendship to his enemies' (*Sa modération dans les victoires, sa clémence à l'egard des vaincus, son amitié vers ses ennemis*).

Artists too continued to transmit favourable images of the emperor after his death. Frans Hogenberg, for instance, made etchings of the Vermeyen cartoons which were published in Cologne c. 1570 and again later. A woodcut of the emperor on horseback circulated in the form of a broadsheet in 1572. A study of some two thousand portraits owned by citizens of Prague mentioned in inventories in the period 1576-1620 reveals some portraits of Charles (though of course they may have been inherited by their owners rather than acquired or commissioned in this period).

In Charles's lifetime it was not yet customary for European monarchs to erect statues to themselves, but after his death he was commemorated in this way. In 1631, a monument to Charles by Scipione Li Volsi was erected in piazza Bologna, Palermo as a companion piece to a statue of Philip IV. In Ghent, as an English traveller noted at the beginning of the eighteenth century, there was a statue of Charles V 'on a high column' in the marketplace. In his defence of the Spanish monarchy, the Italian friar Tommaso Campanella even recommended the erection of a statue of Charles at the South Pole.

Another expression of the Habsburg cult of Charles was the placing of the Titian painting of the emperor at Mühlberg in a prominent place in the palace of the Buen Retiro, while the Vermeyen tapestries of the Tunis campaign were displayed in the main room of the Alcázar of Madrid. In his book of advice for artists, the *Diálogos de la pintura* (1633) Vicente Carducho, discussing possible subjects for history painting, included images of Charles, 'whose victories were excellent and whose battles were mighty'. The piety of the emperor was emphasized in two paintings by Frans Francke II (1581-1642), showing Charles on his knees before a relic of the Virgin Mary, a gown of hers which was kept in the cathedral at Aachen and which the young emperor had viewed at the time of his coronation there. The Neapolitan painter Luca Giordano, who was working in Spain from 1692 onwards, decorated the staircase of the Escorial with an image of Charles and his son adoring St Lawrence, while he evoked the emperor's victories in a series of four paintings in the palace of El Pardo in Madrid.

Other representations of Charles carried rather different messages. At about this time another Spanish artist, Antonio de Pereda (1611-78) used the image of Charles in an allegorical painting of the vanity of human endeavour. In 1647, when the Neapolitans revolted against the Spanish regime, portraits of the emperor were displayed in the street to demonstrate the fundamental loyalty of the rebels and also to remind the government that the city's claim to tax exemption was based on a privilege which Charles had granted them in the previous century.

However, the occasion for the most systematic and elaborate seventeenth-century evocation of Charles V was associated with the state entries into the cities of Antwerp and Ghent, in 1635, of the `cardinal-infant' Ferdinand of Habsburg (1609-41), brother of Philip IV and viceroy of the Netherlands, fresh from his triumphs in the Thirty Years' War. In Antwerp, it was Peter Paul Rubens who designed the entry, which included a portrait of Charles reminiscent of Titian as well as a statue of the emperor, reproduced in the commemorative book, the *Pompa Introitus Ferdinandi*. It is possible that the *Allegory of Charles's V's Abdication*, painted at about this time by the Antwerp artist Frans Francke II, is related to the celebrations for the entry. In Ghent, where the Jesuits planned the festivities, a triumphal arch in honour of Charles V, the *Arcus Caroli*, was erected, with paintings by Gaspar de Crayer (1584-1669). In the iconographical programme, the emperor and the cardinal-infant were viewed in parallel as two crusaders against heresy. A painting by Crayer made for this occasion shows Charles inciting his great-grandson Ferdinand to follow his example.

Charles was indeed taken seriously by some of his descendants as an exemplar of rulership. The emperor Rudolf II, for example, seems to have modelled himself on Charles, especially at the moment when he himself was also thinking of retirement. Rudolf owned a bust of Charles by Leone Leoni and commissioned a portrait of himself from the sculptor Adrian de Vries as a companion-piece to it. Charles's great-grandson Philip IV studied the history of his ancestor as a model to be followed in his own reign.

In Central Europe, S. F. Gariboldi's *Simetria del perfetto Eroe* (1658), written to congratulate Leopold I on his election as Emperor, did so by comparing him to his illustrious ancestor Charles V. Two manuscript accounts of Charles's life and deeds were dedicated to Leopold, an epic poem in Italian by a certain Francesco Maria Santinelli, *Il Carlo Quinto overo Tunesi Racquistata* (1676), and Wenzel Johann von Wallrabe's *Neue historische Beschreibung des Lebens Karls V* (1683). Gregorio Leti's eulogistic four-volume biography, the *Life of the Unconquerable Emperor Charles V*, published in Amsterdam in 1700, was dedicated to one of Leopold's ministers, Dominik Andreas Kaunitz.

However, it was Charles VI (1685-1740) in particular who was presented as a second Charles V. This may have been the point of christening him 'Charles' in the first place, though as the second son of the emperor Leopold he was not expected to rule, and it was only after the death of his elder brother Joseph in 1711 that he succeeded to the throne. However, his name was exploited from the beginning of Charles's reign.

For example, a letter written in 1711 by Karl Gustav Heraeus (1671-1725), inspector of antiquities to the previous emperor, described Charles as 'a second Charles V' (*alter Carolus Quintus*). In a poem written in order to commemorate the Joseph's death, Heraeus made the same point: 'We have a Charles who already equals Charles V' (*Wir haben einen Carl, der schon dem Fünfften gleichet*). References were made once again to the impending return of the golden age. Charles VI revived the feasts of the Order of the Golden Fleece. He commanded the restoration of the Vermeyen cartoons of Charles V's famous campaign in Tunis and he commissioned more tapestries based on these designs. His own expedition to

Gibraltar was seen as a re-enactment of the Tunis campaign
   Like Charles V, Charles VI was compared to Hercules. He took over the famous columnar device, to which the interior decoration of the Hofbibliothek at Vienna, designed by Johan Bernard Fischer von Erlach (1656-1723), makes an obvious reference. The Karlskirche (1715-37), also designed by Fischer, a church which commemorates Vienna's deliverance from plague in 1713, alludes at once to five men named Charles; to Charlemagne, to Charles the Bold of Burgundy, to Charles V, to Charles VI and to his patron saint San Carlo Borromeo, the hero of the Milan plague of 1576. The two great columns flanking the façade once again allude to the famous *impresa* of Charles V. Although he made no explicit reference to Charles VI, when the scholar Hermann von der Hardt dedicated a book about Erasmus, published in 1717, to the memory of Charles V, he was paying implicit homage to the emperor's successor.

Charles as exemplar of reason of state

Outside Charles's former dominions his posthumous image was, as might have been expected, rather less favourable. At best the emperor was praised for his mastery of the art of politics, at worst denounced for his ambition and his use of religion as a tool in the service of reason of state.

   The literature on 'reason of state' which proliferated between the late sixteenth and late seventeenth centuries, often refers to Charles, and in some ways this is appropriate. After all, the official documents of his reign not infrequently justified imperial actions in terms of 'necessity'. In fact, the context of the first recorded use of the phrase *ragion di stato*, by Giovanni Della Casa in 1547, was that of Charles's annexation of Piacenza. According to Sansovino, who presumably intended to pay a compliment, Machiavelli's *Prince* was a favourite book of the emperor's, while a treatise by the humanist Agostino Nifo, plagiarizing Machiavelli's still unpublished text, was presented to the emperor in 1523.

In any case, Giovanni Botero, in his famous treatise *Della Ragion di Stato* (1589), cites a number of the emperor's actions as exemplary. His treatment of the rebellion of Ghent, for example: 'When the emperor Charles V heard that there had been a rising at Ghent he at once posted from Spain to Flanders and put down the trouble at the outset by the authority of his very presence. He punished the rebels and founded a powerful citadel to dominate a city which before had never really capitulated' (Book 5, chapter 9). Again, Charles was praised for the 'outstanding example' he showed in his campaign against the Protestant princes, overcoming 'the fatigues of the body with the greatness of his spirit'.

In similar fashion, in his *Discourses on Tacitus* (1597), the physician Filippo Cavriana compared Charles to the prudent Tiberius in his concern for his troops; praised him for going in person to Flanders, Hungary, Germany and Africa; and declared him 'worthy of eternal fame' (*degno d'eterna lode*) for abdicating, thus showing that after conquering others the emperor was able to conquer himself. The tone of Cavriana, like Botero, is that of eulogy. All the same, to discuss Charles in this way in the context of reason of state implied or at least gave the impression that the emperor made his decisions on political rather than moral grounds and was motivated by interests rather than ideals.

Histories and biographies produced outside the territories of the Habsburgs often went further in this direction. Some of them suggested that the emperor's goals included dominating Europe if not exactly ruling the world. The idea of 'universal monarchy', so important, as we have seen, in Charles's self-presentation, was increasingly turned against him in the seventeenth century. From a divine plan associated with the discovery of America and hopes for the conversion of the infidel, universal monarchy had come to be seen as an all-too-human project for upsetting the balance of power and dominating Europe. Even accounts which were not intended to be hostile now presented Charles as an able and ambitious statesman whose goals were political rather than religious

For example, in his fiercely anti-papal *History of the Council of Trent* (1619), published in Italian in London because it would have been suppressed in Italy, the Venetian friar Paolo Sarpi (1552-1623) presented Charles as the scourge of the papacy. On hearing the news of the sack of Rome and the imprisonment of Clement VII, Charles, according to Sarpi, 'gave many signs of extreme sorrow' (*diede molti segni di grandissimo dolore*). The emperor's reactions would have given a good impression of his piety, Sarpi continued with his customary irony, 'if he had immediately commanded at least the liberation of the pope' (Book 1, chapter 3). Sarpi's Charles is a master of dissimulation. The outward 'signs' or 'appearances' of his intentions could not be trusted, any more than the emperor for his part trusted the outward signs of papal intentions at a time when the popes opposed the holding of a church council while trying to give the impression that they favoured it. In this version of his story, the key to Charles's actions was ambition.

The French in particular went further and presented the adversary of their hero Francis I as a man quite without moral scruples. The most violent expression of French hostility to Charles was probably the one to be found in a pamphlet by the French lawyer Antoine Arnauld, the *Anti-Espagnol* (1592). According to Arnauld, Charles was 'that sworn enemy of our ancestors who lit more fires in Picardy and Provence than the Turk or the Scythian would have done' (*Cet ennemi juré de nos pères qui alluma plus de feux en Picardie et en Provence qu n'eut fait le Turc ou le Scythe*). This condemnation of Charles's invasion of Provence in 1536 was written at the close of the French wars of religion, in which the extreme Catholic faction was supported by Philip II. It is Philip rather than his father who is the real target of the pamphlet.

A generation later, at a time of 'cold war' between France and Spain, François Langlois, seigneur de Fancan (c. 1576-1628), a writer in the service of cardinal Richelieu, claimed in his *Discours salutaire sur l'état présent des affaires de l'Allemagne* (1626), that the King of Spain was attempting to dominate Germany in order to achieve universal monarchy, in the tradition of Charles V ('the first who showed the way', as Fancan put it, 'was Charles V', *Le premier qui a frayé le chemin a été Charles V*). Fancan also made the emperor responsible for the division of Christendom into Catholic and Protestant, on the grounds that he had tolerated heresy in the empire for political reasons and enunciated the notorious principle of *cuius regio eius religio*, 'who rules the region chooses the religion'.

In similar fashion, another official publicist, Daniel de Priézac, in his *Vindiciae Galliae* (1638), noted Charles's desire to dominate Europe and presented the emperor as 'an extraordinary master of dissimulation' (*dissimulationis egregius artifex*: chapter 29). This treatise, written as an answer to the *Mars Gallicus*, an attack on France by the bishop of Ypres, Cornelius Jansen (best known as the author of the treatise which inspired the religious movement of 'Jansenism'), was an apologia for Richelieu's anti-Spanish foreign policy. It is therefore scarcely surprising to find that its central theme was the ambition, irreligion and bad faith of the rulers of Spain.

In the same year that Priézac published his vindication of France, Sandoval's *Vida de Carlos V*, discussed above, was the object of a searching critique by a French philosopher, François La Mothe Le Vayer, in a treatise entitled *Discours de l'histoire* (1638). La Mothe accused Sandoval of what he called a 'calumny' of François I and his ministers, and emphasized what he called the *partialité* of the Spanish historian, for instance his consistent attribution of valour to the Spanish troops alone in their frequent conflicts with the French. La Mothe went on to draw general conclusions about the bias of historians and the unreliability of their versions of the past, and the second edition of his book, emphasising the more general theme, appeared under the bold title 'On the uncertainty of history' (*Du peu de certitude qu'il y a dans l'histoire*, 1668). The first edition, on the other hand, needs to be replaced in the context of the conflict with Spain in the 1630s and La Mothe's own hopes of royal patronage at that time.

Less polemically, at least on the surface, French historians of the later seventeenth century presented Charles as an incarnation of reason of state. For example, in an extended portrait of Charles in his *Histoire de l'Empire* (1684), a French diplomat, Jean de Heiss, stressed the emperor's dissimulation and his ambiguous public utterances. Behind this facade,

Heiss's Charles was a man who 'never stopped dreaming about the strengthening of his dynasty' (*ne laissait pas de songer à l'affermissement de sa maison*). To this end he engaged in intrigues and `all sorts of secret practices' and was even prepared to break his word (as in the notorious case of the imprisonment of the Landgrave of Hesse). No wonder, then, according to Heiss (following Sansovino), that one of Charles's favourite authors was Machiavelli (Book 3, chapter 4).

Antoine Varillas, a historian in the service of Louis XIV, discussed Charles in his *Pratique de l'education des princes* (1684), where he claimed that it was a Frenchman, Chièvres, who had taught the emperor the art of ruling, and he returned to the subject in his *Politique de la maison d'Autriche* (1689). In the latter study, drawing on the literature of reason of state, including the work of Botero, Varillas described the emperor as carrying on 'intrigues' against the liberty of the Empire in the service of his great `project', that of world monarchy. By this time, thanks in part to the efforts of Habsburg pamphleteers, the European ruler who was most widely seen as aiming at universal monarchy was Louis XIV. Hence this French description of Charles may be interpreted as an attempt to divert responsibility from Louis by placing it on the shoulders of the emperor.

This French or Franco-Italian approach was summed up in the entry on Charles in the historical encyclopaedia compiled by Louis Moreri, *Le Grand Dictionnaire Historique* (1683), which gave the verdict that the emperor was 'perhaps a little too subtle and prone to dissimulation, sacrificing everything to his ambition' (*peut-être un peu trop fin et dissimulé, sacrifiant toutes choses à son ambition*). In his more famous *Dictionnaire Historique et Critique* (1697), written precisely as a corrective to Moreri, the Protestant scholar Pierre Bayle agreed with his predecessor at least in emphasizing 'the artifices of a deep policy' (*les artifices d'une profonde politique*), although he could not resist the temptation to ridicule the Spanish Catholics who treated Charles as a saint. Bayle's judgement was that the emperor's reign was 'nothing but a mixture of good and bad fortune' (*son histoire n'est qu'un mélange de bonheur et de malheur*).

In many of the accounts discussed above, the actions of Charles were virtually reduced to illustrations of the maxims of reason of state. Given the prevalence of such an approach to the emperor, it is scarcely surprising to find scholars taking an interest in the so-called 'political testaments', in which, in the course of advising his son Philip, Charles – with or without the aid of his secretaries – made his views explicit and put them on paper. Sandoval, for instance, printed the testament of 1548 as a document illustrating the life of the emperor which he published in 1604-6. In 1699, Charles's testament was published independently, in a French translation by Antoine Tessier, under the title of *Instructions de Charles V à Philippe II*. This form of publication, following the circulation of manuscript copies, suggests that the text was now intended, like earlier commentaries on Tacitus, to teach the art of politics, this time in a more up-to-date form. The book was reprinted in 1700, and again in 1788.

In English too a text claiming to be the *Advice of Charles V to his son Philip II* was published in 1670. To anyone familiar with the laconic prose of Charles's testaments, the prolix and Polonius-like moralizing of the emperor in this text will sound strange indeed: 'choose the way of sweetness and clemency to make your throne durable, rather than that of violence and rigour to render yourself more absolute ... the first step to make yourself rich is to make your people so'. It does not seem unreasonable to suggest that at a time when Louis XIV was making himself an absolute monarch and threatening to disrupt the balance of power, Charles, the old enemy of the French, was being redefined by the English as his opposite.

Charles V in the Enlightenment

Despite his claim to be offering an account of the progress of manners and of the human mind, rather than a traditional political history, Voltaire devoted a chapter to the emperor in his *Essai sur les Moeurs* (1751). Dismissing as 'chimerical' the idea of universal monarchy attributed to Charles, and aware of the problems he faced, the 'precipices' which surrounded him', Voltaire's verdict emphasized the *gloire* of the man who 'always played the main part on the European stage ... no emperor since Charlemagne had made such an impression as Charles V did' (*joua toujours le premier rôle sur le théâtre de l'Europe ... nul empereur depuis Charlemagne n'eut tant d'éclat que Charles-Quint*).

However, the most influential eighteenth-century image of the emperor was the work of a Scotsman, William Robertson (1721-93), principal of the University of Edinburgh and a leading figure of the Scottish Enlightenment.

The reasons for Robertson's decision to write a massive *History of the Reign of the Emperor Charles V*, first published in 1769, are not immediately obvious. Indeed, Robertson's friend the philosopher-historian David Hume tried to dissuade him from the project, in a letter written in 1759, on the grounds that 'your hero ... is not very interesting'. Why should a Scottish Protestant clergyman who had made his reputation by publishing a history of Scotland choose this particular topic for his second book?

One possibility is that Robertson was thinking of turning his national reputation into an international one by choosing a subject with a continental appeal. Another is suggested by the dedication to King George III, which suggests in a tactful way that Robertson, like Gibbon, was interested in the topical theme of the decline of empire: 'What reflections the reign of the emperor Charles V may suggest to Your Majesty it becomes not me to conjecture'. To this we may add a natural concern on the part of the Moderator of the Church of Scotland with the Protestant Reformation, to which Robertson devotes what he calls a 'digression' of fifty-five pages. Again, like other figures in the Scottish Enlightenment, his friend Adam Smith, for example, Robertson was interested in economic, social and political systems. Writing about Charles V gave him an opportunity to discuss the European balance of power and more generally the decline of feudalism and the rise of the modern world, major themes in his famous introductory section on 'the progress of society in Europe'. Finally, the topic may have attracted Robertson by its globality. He went on to write a *History of America* (1777), which praised Charles for his *New Laws* concerning the Indies.

Robertson had a few good things to say about the emperor, praising his 'capacious and decisive judgement', for example, his 'manly address', 'the dignity of his character' and 'the grandeur of his views'. All the same, the historian's final verdict was essentially a negative one. According to Robertson, a northern Protestant in an age in which the elites were increasingly attracted by sincerity and repelled by artifice, Charles was simply too skilful at self-representation, or to put the matter more bluntly, at 'dissimulation'. The emperor's 'artful address', notably in 'assuming' the manners of his Spanish subjects, was the subject of more than one critical comment on the part of his historian. Charles's 'pretensions to moderation' were dismissed as nothing but window-dressing, while his negative reaction to the sack of Rome by his troops was described, following Sarpi, as 'hypocritical'.

Indeed, according to Robertson, Charles was a man 'but little under the influence of religious considerations', although he tried to cover his actions with 'the specious veil of religion'. His 'composed and regular deportment' was a kind of mask 'admirably adapted to conceal his own passions'. What lay behind the mask? Robertson had little doubt about the answer to this question. For Charles, 'Ambition ... was the ruling passion in his mind'. This ambition or 'love of power' was 'boundless', it was 'insatiable', and at times, when the emperor was 'intoxicated with success', his true motives broke through the mask or veil. In other words the Scottish academic Robertson was essentially reproducing the 'reason of state' view of Charles which had been elaborated in the sixteenth and seventeenth centuries by a series of French and Italian political writers.

From the publishing point of view, it was Hume who was mistaken about the potential interest of the subject, while Robertson was vindicated. He received an advance of £3, 500 from his publisher, 'the greatest price' (once again according to Hume) `that was ever known to be given for any book'.

The first edition consisted of four thousand copies, of which almost three thousand were sold in four months (despite the high price for the period of two pounds, twelve shillings and sixpence). By 1817 the book had reached its fourteenth edition, and this without counting the unauthorized versions which were produced in Dublin and Philadelphia.

Robertson's *Charles V* also received a warm reception in Germany, in France (where one reviewer compared the author to Montesquieu and Voltaire), and elsewhere. The French translation appeared in 1771, a version frequently reprinted in the course of the nineteenth century. The first German edition was published in 1770-1 and the second in 1779. Robertson's book was also translated into Russian (1775-8), Italian (1835), Arabic (1842) and Spanish (1846).

The view of Charles presented by Robertson was reiterated by other British writers, notably Edward Gibbon and William Coxe. In the thirteenth chapter of his famous *Decline and Fall of the Roman Empire* (1776-89), Gibbon compared the retirement of Charles and Diocletian and noted 'the very striking resemblance between the characters of the two emperors, whose political abilities were superior to their military genius and whose specious virtues were much less the effect of nature than of art'. William Coxe (1747-1828), a clergyman who had discovered Central Europe in the course of taking young aristocrats on the Grand Tour, published a *History of the House of Austria* (1807) in which he described Charles as a ruler of 'foresight, art and sagacity' who 'excelled in whatever he undertook', but also as a man with serious moral defects, including 'duplicity', a 'mean spirit of revenge', and an 'insatiable thirst of power'.

A similarly negative view of Charles as despot emerges

from the pages of the poet Friedrich Schiller (1759-1805). In his *Geschichte des Abfalls der Vereinigte Niederlande von der Spanische Regierung* (1788), Schiller presented the revolt of the Netherlands as a struggle between freedom and absolutism, the latter incarnated in the person of the emperor. Schiller referred to the revolt of the Netherlands as a 'great revolution' (the poet doubtless had the recent American Revolution in mind), and he emphasised the theme of liberty, whether civic (*bürgerlichen Freiheit*) or intellectual (*Gewissensfreiheit*). Indeed, the first edition of this book displayed on the titlepage a hat of liberty of the kind to be found on the tomb of William the Silent in Delft.

In similar fashion, although he placed more emphasis on religion, the North American John Lothrop Motley (1814-77), a strong supporter of Protestantism and liberty, and author of *The Rise of the Dutch Republic* (1856), argued that the emperor had regarded the Netherlands 'merely as a treasury' and condemned him for having planted there the 'diabolical institution' of the Inquisition. He had praise for Charles as a 'military genius' and a 'shrewd' politician. On the other hand, Motley's moral judgement on the emperor was severe. Charles was described as a man who 'believed in nothing', 'entirely without chivalry', and 'as false as water'.

In contrast, the Anglican bishop and constitutional historian William Stubbs (1825-1901), in a course of lectures on European history (posthumously published in book form in 1904), presented a more positive view of the emperor. Criticizing Motley on the grounds that Charles had as much chivalry as anyone else in his time, and Robertson for viewing Charles as 'a mere machine on whose wooden framework you can calculate exactly the mechanical effects of every blow of fortune', Stubbs claimed that Charles was not only a 'tough and wiry' character but also a great ruler. To support his claim, the historian offered two arguments. In the first place, Charles 'had no minister who ruled him'. In the second place, 'only a great sovereign could have kept together the empire that Charles V did keep together for forty years'.

National images

By the time of Motley the so-called Rankean 'revolution' in historical writing had occurred, in other words the discovery of archives. Where Robertson, for example, had built his interpretation on the foundation of earlier narratives (Sleidan, for instance, Sarpi, and even the unreliable Leti), Leopold von Ranke (1795-1886) made use of at least some documentary sources, most notably the reports of the Venetian ambassadors to the imperial court. Ranke's first sketch of Charles, in a book about *The Ottoman and Spanish Empires* (1827), used and quoted these sources to good effect, constructing from the reports an image of the emperor as hard-working, well-informed, and decisive, even obstinate at times – as Charles himself was the first to admit – but also slow to make up his mind, like his son Philip, because he insisted on weighing with care the arguments for and against a particular course of action.

The editing of primary sources was an important part of the new or Rankean approach to the past. In the case of Charles, for instance, important contributions were made by Louis-Prosper Gachard (1800-85), archivist-general of the Kingdom of Belgium, who carried out research in Simancas in 1843-4.

The letters of Guillaume van Male, which offered an unusually intimate view of the emperor's last years, were printed in 1843. The German scholar Karl Lanz published an edition of the official correspondence of the emperor in three volumes (1844-6). Another German scholar, Gotthilf Heine, edited the letters written to Charles by his confessor (1848). Gachard himself published letters which described the emperor's retirement (1854-5). The Belgian scholar Baron Joseph Kervyn de Lettenhove published Charles's memoirs (1862).

Another major feature of the historical writing of this period was an increasing awareness of the twin dangers of anachronism and partiality. Where earlier French historians had virtually taken it for granted, as we have seen, that Charles V's goal was the establishment of universal monarchy, Auguste Mignet (1796-1884), in a study of the rivalry between Charles and Francis I, argued that this aspiration could no more have been conceived by Charles than it could have been realized. Whether or not Mignet's conclusion was correct, he had raised a fundamental question. If they are defined in more precise terms than 'power' or 'security', then the goals of rulers and other politicians cannot be assumed to have been the same in every period in history.

Again, discussing the question of Charles's severity, the Belgian historian Alexandre Henne claimed that he was not cruel 'by the standards of his time' (*aux yeux de son siècle*). Henne prided himself on his objectivity and declared in the preface to his monograph on the emperor that 'I have searched for truth without passion, prejudice or party spirit' (*j'ai recherché la vérité sans passion, sans idée préconçue, sans esprit de parti*).

Despite the newly-published documents, however, and

the typically nineteenth-century claims to objectivity and the avoiding of anachronism, differences in interpretation often followed national lines, whether German, Spanish or Belgian. The international Charles of the more cosmopolitan eighteenth century was now followed by a national one.

Ranke's second portrait of Charles forms part of his *German History* (1839-47). Ranke was careful to point out that the house of Burgundy had nothing in common with national movements, and that German interests were not central to Charles's political strategies. On the other hand, in the age of German unification it was virtually inevitable that Germans would see Charles as a great German leader, comparable to other national heroes such as Luther and Bismarck.

The most famous modern study of Charles is that of Brandi. Karl Brandi (1868-1946), was a Protestant who emphasised both German affairs and the Reformation in his *Kaiser Karl V* (1937), but also presented the emperor as a statesman who did much to achieve European unity without conquest. In its sixth German edition by 1961, and translated into English, French, Spanish, Italian and Dutch, this book has probably done more than any other to shape the twentieth-century image of the emperor.

Brandi's work was based on some thirty years' pursuit of new sources, scattered over the archives of Europe. It made a considerable effort to present events as the emperor and his advisers would have seen them at the time. However, the book is perhaps most important and original in its stress on what the author calls the 'inner life' of the emperor, in other words his intellectual development from the adolescent who followed the advice of Chièvres and Gattinara to the self-reliant ruler of the period after 1530. As the author explained in his preface, 'I have sought ... to live over, step by step, with the Emperor, the gradual processes of his extraordinary career, with all its puzzling delays, crises, hopes and wearinesses. I have not sought to vindicate the Emperor's actions nor to paint the portrait of a hero, but rather to draw the features of a man and a ruler, with his frailties and his virtues'.

It would be an over-simplification to suggest that all earlier writers had presented the emperor's personality as completely static. Already in the seventeenth century, Sarpi, for instance, had claimed that Charles became more ambitious after the Tunis campaign, while Varillas had posed the question whether or not the emperor's actions became bolder after the battle of Pavia. All the same, Brandi's emphasis on Charles's inner development is an essentially new one. His insights were achieved by displacing attention from the Venetian reports favoured by Ranke (a rather literary kind of document), and even from the texts of official decrees. Brandi's favourite sources, on the other hand, were the draft memoranda which revealed by their very formlessness the way in which imperial policies gradually developed. The historian took his readers back into the workshop or rather into the 'think tank' of the emperor.

The picture of the emperor painted by Brandi was a balanced one. He may have given disproportionate space to events in the German-speaking part of the emperor's dominions, but he placed these events firmly in their international context. He presented Charles as a man who was or at least became an able politician, even if he was never a great leader. By contrast, Peter Rassow (1889-1961), who devoted two books to the emperor, one produced before and the other after the Second World War, sometimes wrote of Charles as a kind of superman, a world-historical leader endowed with 'an enormous force of will' and 'extraordinary intelligence'.

Rassow's romantic-Hegelian interpretation of the emperor makes an even more striking contrast with that of his American contemporary Royall Tyler (1884-1953), a historian of Spanish art before he turned to the biography of the emperor in a study published posthumously in 1956. Tyler's Charles is unusually human and sympathetic, well aware that he did not control events, although 'For a thousand years, from Charlemagne to Napoleon, no other ruler mattered so much to Christendom'. The emperor is portrayed as a man with a strong sense of duty, hard-working, 'a frail unassuming little man, humorously aware of his physical peculiarities ... kind and considerate ... undaunted in adversity, undazzled by success' (the stoic theme of constancy does not seem to have lost its power to attract the biographer).

The Spaniards by contrast, offered an interpretation of the emperor as essentially Spanish. Antonio Cánovas del Castillo (1828-97), who was both historian and statesman, described Charles as 'Spanish before everything' (*español ante todo*). Ramón Menéndez Pidal (1869-1968), President of the Spanish Academy, emphasised the Spanish origins of the imperial idea. He contrasted the image of the emperor as crusader, put forward by Pedro Mota, for example, with the Italian Gattinara's concept of world monarchy. According to Don Ramón it was not Gattinara, as many scholars had thought, but the Spaniard Antonio de Guevara who had written the famous speech which Charles delivered at Madrid in 1528.

The Belgian scholars Reiffenberg, Henne and Gachard also

offered an extremely positive view of the emperor, as well as emphasising his special relation to the Low Countries. Baron Frédéric de Reiffenberg (1795-1850) criticized those who have 'tried to minimize his abilities as a ruler' (*cherché à le rabaisser comme souverain*). On the contrary, according to Reiffenberg, `Charles V is one of the select band of princes who, contrary to the laws of common perspective, become greater as they recede in time ... we admire more and more the genius of the monarch who established the balance of power' (*Charles-Quint est du petit nombre des princes qui, contre les lois de l'optique vulgaire, grandissent en avançant dans la postérité ... on admire davantage le génie de cet monarque qui créa la politique de l'équilibre*). 'What tact, what skill, what an extraordinarily broad vision, what prodigious activity' (*Quel tact, quelle adresse, quelle immensité de coup d'oeuil, quelle activité prodigieuse*). Reiffenberg also described the emperor as 'a Fleming in the full sense of the term' (*un Flamand, dans toute la force du terme*).

Alexandre Henne (1812-96) produced a ten-volume *Histoire du Règne de Charles V en Belgique* (1858-60), explaining to his readers that despite his impartiality he was concerned with 'our national honour'. In the conclusion to this work Henne presented Charles as a great man, indeed a political 'genius', 'wide-ranging and penetrating' (*vaste et profonde*) 'who was able to go to the heart of a complicated matter in a moment and to see the whole in the details' (*il embrassait d'un coup d'oeuil l'ensemble des combinaisons les plus compliqués*). On the other hand, Henne allowed himself to doubt whether Charles added anything to civilization, progress or the happiness of nations.

Gachard was less ambivalent about the emperor than his colleague. In the long article on the emperor which he wrote for the *Biographie Nationale de Belgique*, he praised the constancy and energy of Charles's character. He defended the emperor – as Braudel would defend Charles's son Philip – against the charge of unnecessary slowness of decision: `the point of this slowness was that he wanted to consider affairs with extreme care and from different points of view' (*cette lenteur tenait à ce qu'il voulait considérer minutieusement les affaires sous leurs diverses faces*). Gachard noted that Charles was a lover of literature and the arts, and ended by quoting the verdict of the Venetian ambassador Tiepolo to the effect that Charles was the greatest emperor of Christendom since Charlemagne. This judgement, concluded Gachard, 'has been ratified by history'.

Popular images

The historian's Charles is not, of course, the only posthumous Charles. The emperor has long had a place in popular imagination, in some parts of Europe at least. In the nineteenth century, the rise of interest in `folklore' led to systematic collection of popular oral traditions. The *Sagen* published by the famous German philologist Jacob Grimm (1785-1863) for example, include one story, from Hesse, about Charles and his army sinking at Odenburg, and another (no. 28), of Charles, like his ancestor and namesake Charlemagne, not dead but asleep, his beard growing through a stone table, waiting for the moment of his return as the last world emperor. As so often happens in oral tradition, different historical figures have been amalgamated in this story, in a process akin to what Freud, in his famous interpretation of dreams, called 'condensation'.

This vision of Charles as a superhuman hero has as its complementary opposite a view of him as a man of the people, who is sometimes mistaken for an ordinary person. An early example of this view comes from an Italian manuscript of the end of the sixteenth century which presented the emperor quite literally with his hose down, having gone into a garden to relieve himself and being pursued by the owner, an old lady with a stick, who tells him to get out before the emperor arrives.

The southern Netherlands is particularly rich in folklore of this kind, some of which found its way into print in the seventeenth and eighteenth centuries. In *Les actions héroiques et plaisantes de l'empereur Charles V* (discussed above), a text which went through at least thirteen editions in Flemish and French between 1675 and 1800, the emperor is presented as both simple and accessible. In this text his plain clothes, which had once shocked the Venetian ambassadors, bear witness to his modesty. His piety is illustrated by an engraving in which the emperor carries a crucifix. The reader also learns that Charles 'listened to the rich and the poor without making any distinction between them (*écoutait les riches et les pauvres sans distinction*).

As evidence of his common touch we read of the emperor's encounters with a cobbler, a grocer, a landlady, a sacristan and a number of peasants, including a meeting near Brussels with a peasant who does not recognise him and asks Charles to hold a lantern while he takes a pee. The story is first recorded in a sixteenth-century chronicle, and it would be told again in a poem by Prudens van Duyse (1804-59), as well as in a vaudeville, first played in Ghent in 1841, by Hippoliet van Peene (1811-64). The continuing circulation of the story is evidence of the popular appeal of both the jest and its hero the emperor.

The tale of the lantern was far from the only funny story in circulation about `Keizer Karel', as he was affectionately described in the Spanish Netherlands. The Jesuit Antoine de Balinghem (1571-1630), in his *Après-dinées* (1615), told the story of Charles in Ghent finding a drunkard asleep and dressing him as a prince, as in the prologue to Shakespeare's *Midsummer Night's Dream*. Another story is that of Charles and the cobbler who refuses to work on the day of his patron Saint Crispin. Another is that of the peasant who offers the emperor a turnip and is rewarded with eight hundred crowns.

Yet another famous anecdote is that of the innkeeper offering Charles a mug of beer, but holding the mug by the handle, so that it was difficult for the emperor to take it. Charles gave him a gold coin to allow him to buy a mug with two handles. The next time the emperor asked for a drink, the innkeeper offered him the new mug, but held both handles. Charles therefore ended by giving the man another gold coin to buy a mug with three handles. The story allows us to place the image of Charles on a contemporary beer-mat in a longer tradition. The dramatist Michel de Ghelderode (1898-1962) also drew on these popular traditions in his play *Le perroquet de Charles-Quint* (1934), in which the emperor's pet parrot Spiridon escapes but is recaptured by a peasant who is rewarded with the office of governor of the imperial clocks. Charles is portrayed as an ordinary human being capable of bursting into laughter or walking about his palace in his night-shirt.

Why Charles rather than another ruler should have become a popular hero after his death, especially in the southern Netherlands, is an intriguing question. It is relevant but surely insufficient to say that the emperor was indeed able to communicate with ordinary people or even that he liked jokes. In Yuste one day, according to the Venetian ambassador, Charles complained to his majordomo that the food was tasteless. On receiving the reply that nothing would satisfy him but 'clock soup', the emperor exploded with laughter.

In my own opinion, the posthumous reputation of rulers has relatively little to do with their personalities but is shaped largely by subsequent events. Part of the explanation of Charles's later popularity, as I have already tried to suggest, is that the disaster of civil war in the Netherlands followed so soon after his abdication and death. When the seventeen provinces were divided into the Dutch Republic and the Spanish Netherlands, the cult of Charles may also have become a means for the people of the south to define themselves collectively against the northerners.

The genuine contrast between the popular memories of Charles in the southern Netherlands and elsewhere in his dominions must not be exaggerated. In Spain too some stories of this kind were told about the emperor, notably in Zúñiga's comic chronicle (discussed above), a text which circulated in manuscript in the sixteenth century. Even La Roca's generally dignified and serious *Epitome* of 1622 tells a story about the emperor joking with his barber about his funeral.

However, generally speaking, Charles's image in Spain was a more serious one, at least in the historical dramas of the so-called 'golden age', in which the emperor was frequently represented. The late sixteenth and early seventeenth century were a time when the public theatre, appealing to a wide audience ranging from nobles to apprentices, flourished in Madrid and other Spanish cities, just as it did in Elizabethan and Jacobean London.

The tradition of putting the emperor on the stage apparently began with Juan de la Cueva (1550-1609), whose play *El Sacro de Roma* included a scene showing Charles's coronation in Bologna. It continued with Francisco Augustín Tárrega (1554-1602), whose *El Cerco de Pavia* represented the capture of Francis I; and Cristóbal de Monroy y Silva (1612-49), whose play *La batalla de Pavia* followed the model of Tárrega. Bartolomé de Salazar y Luna's *Los dos monarcas de Europa* put Clement VII and the emperor on stage together, and, like Cueva's play, represented the imperial coronation. Diego Jiménez de Encisco (1585-1634) turned the spotlight on the emperor in *La Mayor Hazaña del Emperador Carlos Quinto*. This play includes scenes showing Charles's abdication and his retirement to Yuste, but its climax is the moment when a ghost appears to tell the emperor that 'the greatest exploit is to know how to die'.

In his long and productive career, the greatest Spanish dramatist of the period, Felix Lope de Vega Carpio (1562-1635), devoted several plays to the life of the emperor, basing himself in part on stories told in the biography by Ulloa and the history by Sandoval. *El valiente Céspedes*, for example, represents the battle of Mühlberg. *Carlos V en Francia*, which was played at court in 1623, makes much of the dramatic contrast between the lively and extroverted Francis I and the *gravedad* of the emperor at the time of their meeting at Aigues-Mortes. *La mayor desgracia de Carlos V* is bold enough to represent the Algerian campaign, explaining its failure by witchcraft and showing the emperor defying his ill fortune and going on – with a cheerful reversal of chronology – to triumph at Tunis.

Lope de Vega's Charles is a moral giant. A minor character speaks on one occasion of his superhuman grandeur (*grandezas más que humanas*). On occasion, however, Lope also presents Charles, as in the Flemish jest-books, as a ruler close to the people. Displaying the excellent memory for which Luis de Avila and others had praised him, Charles is shown here in the act of recognising in Algeria a soldier who had served him well – reversing chronology again – in the war against the German Protestant princes.

The sayings of the emperor

Collections of the sayings as well as the deeds of famous people were a well-loved literary genre at this time, and one of the seventeenth-century biographies of Charles bore the title *Les mots et les belles actions de l'empereur Charles V*. Dicta attributed to the emperor in texts of the sixteenth and seventeenth century may not have been close to reality but at least they testify clearly to the process of mythification.

For example, the diplomat-author Baldassare Castiglione was supposed to have been described by Charles as 'one of the finest gentlemen in the world' (*uno do los mejores caballeros del mundo*). On the death of Sir Thomas More, the emperor's comment was that 'We would rather have lost the best city of our dominions than have lost such a worthy councillor'. At the battle of Mühlberg (according to the historians Alfonso Ulloa and Juan Ochoa), Charles improved on Caesar and declared that 'I came, I saw, and God conquered (*Vine y Vi y Dios Vencio*). On the death of his trusted councillor cardinal Tavera, who had administered Spain in his absence, Charles is reported to have said that 'I have lost an old man who kept the kingdoms of Spain in order for me with his walking-stick' (*Se me ha muerto un viejecito que me tenía sosegados los reinos de España con su báculo*).

When his nobles complained that he spent hours with the Italian historian Francesco Guicciardini, Charles is supposed to have replied that 'he could in an instant create a hundred grandees, but that only God could make a Guicciardini'. His admiration for Titian is revealed in a story told by Carlo Ridolfi in *Le Meraviglie dell'Arte* (1648). One one occasion, when Titian was painting the emperor's portrait, he dropped his brush and the emperor picked it up. Titian's comment was 'Sire, I do not merit such an honour'. Charles's reply was that 'Titian is worthy of being served by Caesar'.

On the other hand, Charles is supposed to have detested Martin Luther. According to a German story, the Spaniards asked the emperor for Luther's body after his death in order to burn it, but Charles refused, saying 'Leave him in peace. I don't want to see him again, I saw enough of him at Worms'. The Englishman Robert Dallington's *Survey of Tuscany* (1601) recorded two witticisms of the emperor. Florence he described as 'a city which should only be shown on holy days'. As for its cathedral, so colourfully decorated on the outside, Charles's comment was 'Pity it had not a mantle to keep it from foul weather'.

One of the most memorable remarks attributed to Charles expresses the views of this polyglot ruler on language. In the classic version, recorded in print in the mid-seventeenth century by the French critic Dominique Bouhours, Charles said 'that if he wanted to speak to ladies, he would speak Italian; that if he wanted to speak to men, he would speak French; that if he wanted to speak to his horse, he would speak German; but that if he wanted to speak to God, he would speak Spanish (*que s'il vouloit parler aux dames, il parleroit Italien; que s'il vouloit parler aux hommes, il parleroit François; que s'il vouloit parler à son cheval, il parleroit Allemand; mais que s'il vouloit parler à Dieu, il parleroit Espagnol*). In the earliest known version (in a text by the Italian G. Fabrizi, published in 1601), of this widespread story, which comes in many variants, Charles 'used to say, that he spoke Spanish to his God, Italian to courtiers, French to his ladies and Dutch to his horse'.

Alas, all that Charles is known to have said on the subject, in his political testament, is much more conventional; that it was necessary for Prince Philip to learn languages and that 'Latin is indispensable, French very important'. The emperor's point was improved by the sixteenth-century French writer the Seigneur de Brantôme into the saying, 'The more languages one knows, the more lives one has' (*Autant de langues on possède, autant de fois on est homme*).

The domestication of Charles V

The printed accounts discussed above probably record stories which had been circulating by word of mouth. The image of Charles in nineteenth-century literature, essentially for middle-class readers, makes a strong contrast to this oral tradition. Where the Charles of oral tradition was either superhuman or a man of the people, nineteenth-century literature showed an increasing concern for the domestic, private or inner life of the emperor.

For example, a collection of letters describing Charles's last years were published in 1843 under the title of *Lettres sur la vie intérieure de l'empereur*. An Englishman with an interest in Spanish art, Sir William Stirling (later Stirling-Maxwell, 1818-78), devoted a book to what he called *The Cloister Life of Charles V* (1852), following the emperor's retirement to the monastery at Yuste. Stirling offered a vivid description of the private Charles, the everyday life of the retired emperor, his health, his hobbies, notably his interest in clocks, and his taste in food, art, books and music, of which he was particularly fond.

The nineteenth-century was also the age of the rise of historical painting for a middle-class public, which viewed these works in public galleries, and especially in annual exhibitions. Here too we can detect an interest in Charles the man as well as the emperor, notably in the case of a painting by Jan van Beers, 'Charles V as a child' (1879). His abdication, another revelation of the man behind the official facade, was painted more than once: by Philippe van Bree, for instance, c. 1824, and by Louis Gallait (1841). It was to this latter artist that Alexandre Henne dedicated his biography of the emperor. A number of Spanish artists, including Joaquín Agrasot y Juan (1836-1919), painted the arrival of Charles at Yuste or scenes from his retirement there.

The historian Simon Schama has written about what he calls the 'domestication of majesty' in royal portraits of the nineteenth century. Louis Philippe, Queen Victoria and other monarchs were increasingly presented in domestic settings, thus reducing the social distance between themselves and the viewers, their subjects, in a manner considered appropriate for a democratic monarchy. This domestication appears to have been projected back onto the past. In art and literature alike, some of the new representations of Charles as a private individual fit this model. Even when participating in a public event such giving audience to Francisco Pizarro, the emperor was presented in an engraving by Angel Lizcano y Esteban in an informal manner, with his gouty feet resting on a cushion.

Public themes did not disappear altogether. Religious values help explain the choice of 'Charles standing by the grave of Luther', or Nicaise de Keyer's 'Charles V frees christian slaves in Tunis' (1873), in which the emperor appears as a kind of saviour, reminiscent of the famous image of Napoleon in the hospital in Jaffa. National or civic sentiment was expressed in 'Charles V enters Antwerp' (1877-8), by the Austrian painter Hans Makart (1840-84). In similar fashion, Karel Miry (1823-89), one of the first Belgian composers to set texts in Flemish, including the music for 'De vlaamse leeuw', also composed an opera about the emperor. The opera *Karl V* by Ernst Krenek, commissioned by the Vienna State Opera House in the 1930s, had an even more obvious political meaning. Composed at a time when Hitler was planning to incorporate the country into his Reich, the opera was given a consciously Austrian and Catholic flavour. The première – in 1938 – took place not in Vienna but in Prague.

In Spain, Charles's son Philip, known as 'the wise' (*Felipe el prudente*) has been more successful than his father in appealing to the popular imagination. In the German-speaking world, Charles has had to compete with other royal heroes such as Charlemagne and the emperor Frederick. Charles's greatest posthumous success has been in the land of his birth, the Low Countries, especially Belgium. However, in the twentieth century the national image of Charles has been increasingly replaced by an international one.

Supranational perspectives

As we have seen, Charles has been presented in a number of different and indeed incompatible ways. He has been described as an idealist (the defender of Christendom, or as the English historian Frances Yates once described him, a 'pious dreamer'), but also as an opportunist guided only by reason of state. He has been variously viewed as Spanish, German or Flemish at heart. For some, he makes an obvious example of a Renaissance prince who appreciated the paintings of Titian, was on friendly terms with Castiglione, and took some interest in classical antiquity, at least in imperial Rome. For others, like Peter Rassow, Charles was 'The last emperor of the Middle Ages', essentially concerned with the peace and unity of Christendom and what Rassow calls 'die sakrale Auffassung vom Kaisertum'. His campaigns in North Africa have been described as crusades. His challenge to Francis I to meet him in single combat, like his interest in the romance *Le chevalier délibéré*, have often been cited to support the argument that Charles's values were fundamentally those of late medieval chivalry. As we have already seen, many of these interpretations have a long history.

However, three views of the emperor are particularly characteristic of the twentieth century. The first, predictable in a century of sociology and social history, is that Charles was unimportant, in the sense of having little or no influence on the course of events. In his *Outline of History* (1920), for instance, the English writer H. G. Wells, better known as a novelist, dismissed the emperor as 'a man of commonplace abilities and melancholy temperament ... who was, through no fault of his own, to become the focus of the accumulating stresses of Europe. The historian must give him a quite unmerited and accidental prominence'.

Again, in the third volume (1907) of his *Histoire de Belgique*, Henri Pirenne (1862-1935), combining a focus on Belgium with a characteristically wide vision of Europe, emphasized the way in which the emperor's global policies were imposed on him by 'the acquisition of the empire, the declared hostility of Francis I, and the coming of the Reformation' (*L'acquisition de l'empire, l'hostilité déclarée de François I, l'apparition de la Réforme lui imposent une politique mondiale*). Pirenne's term 'imposed' is a significant one, and it brings his image of the emperor close to that of Fernand Braudel, who was notorious for his view of the historical unimportance of mere individuals and events.

In his famous book *La Méditerranée et le monde méditerranéen à l'époque de Philippe II* (1949), Braudel dismissed Charles in a single cryptic sentence as 'an accident calculated, prepared and desired by Spain' (*un hasard calculé, préparé, voulu d'Espagne*). However, Braudel went on to publish a more sympathetic essay on Charles (in Italian, in 1965), beginning with a section headed 'the place of chance less important than it is usually said to be' (*La part du hasard moins grande qu'on ne le dit d'ordinaire*), and continuing with the claim that Charles was not the 'prisoner' of a policy or an imperial idea. In an article of 1958 on Charles's finances, Braudel had already rejected economic interpretations of the emperor's policies and put forward a more pluralistic view. All the same, it is the author's view of Charles as accident or prisoner that is most clearly remembered, precisely because it fits more easily into the well-known Braudelian philosophy of history.

In similar fashion, Ramón Carande, in his classic study *Carlos V y sus banqueros* (1967) emphasized the financial constraints on the emperor, the inevitable and recurrent problems of debt and credit. Braudel's follower Pierre Chaunu devoted a book to *L'Espagne de Charles V* (1973) in which the emperor is virtually invisible, hidden behind a screen of economic and social 'structures' and 'conjunctures'. At about the same time, another disciple of Braudel, the Marxist Immanuel Wallerstein, in *The Modern World-System* (1974), argued that Charles V's efforts to dominate Europe had negative results on Spain and the cities of Flanders, Germany and North Italy, as well as on the dynasties of merchants who 'linked their fate to empire'. In the long run, the emperor's policies helped prepare the way for a new 'world economy' in which these areas became increasingly peripheral, while the Dutch and English moved towards the centre.

The second major twentieth-century development is that the national or nationalist image of Charles has, gradually but generally, been replaced by a view which is broader though no less influenced by contemporary politics, the politics of the Common Market and the European Union (the emperor's early years based in Brussels and his international team of councillors, to say nothing about the *écu*, make the parallel between past and present virtually irresistible). Where earlier Spanish historians emphasized the Spanishness of the emperor, the verdict of Manuel Fernández Alvarez, in a study published in a British series in 1975, is that Charles 'belonged to none of his kingdoms'. Charles is now presented more and more often as a good European, especially in studies intended for non-academic readers.

This 'European' view of the emperor goes back at least as far as the 1930s. Krenek's opera, mentioned above, is one sign among others that the problems of Central Europe after 1918, especially the problems of conflicting nationalisms, were already encouraging a certain nostalgia for the international Habsburg Empire, Charles V included. The Spanish scholar Ramón Menéndez Pidal, for all his emphasis on the Spanish origins of the imperial idea, also argued in 1937 that 'Charles was the politician who believed most sincerely and most firmly in European unity' (*Carlos V fué el político que más sincera y firmemente creyó en la unidad europea*).

A similar point was made at greater length and with rather less discretion by D. B. Wyndham Lewis (1891-1969), in a biography which appeared in the USA under the title *Charles of Europe* (1931). Wyndham Lewis, a British convert to Catholicism (like his friend the writer G. K. Chesterton), presented Charles as 'the champion of the old European Idea, which happens now to be extremely modern'. By this he meant the idea of a Christian commonwealth, threatened in Charles's time by 'the disintegrating influences of Luther and his rivals within and the onslaught of the Turks from without'. After the Second World War, the writer Gertrude Schwarzenfeld gave a description of her travels in Spain the title 'Charles V the Ancestor of Europe' (*Karl V Ahnherr Europas*, 1954). In a speech delivered on 3 July 1962, Charles De Gaulle described European union as a dream of Charles V's, and he returned to the theme in his memoirs, *Le renouveau* (1970), in which he compared Charles's efforts for union with those of Charlemagne and Napoleon. Again, in the foreword to a study published in 1967, Otto von Habsburg described Charles's idea of European unity as an 'anticipation' of 'today', while the Belgian historian Charles Terlinden subtitled his biography of Charles, published in 1978, 'The Emperor Charles V, Forerunner of the Idea of Europe'.

In such discussions it is essential to avoid a narrow definition of Europe and to remember that Charles's titles included those of the ruler of Hungary and Croatia as well as Spain, the Netherlands, Germany and parts of Italy. As John Headley puts it, we need to 'attain a supranational perspective' in order to study a multicultural empire which was administered in Latin, French, Flemish, German, Spanish and Italian. It is possible that a post-national age like our own, torn between regional revivals and globalization, is well placed to understand a pre-national age in which the phrase 'universal monarchy' was taken seriously by publicists and even by politicians. All the same, there remains a disquieting tendency to use Charles, like Charlemagne, as a symbol of Europe, more especially of a particular Europe, that of the European Union. As Peter Rassow once remarked, it is anachronistic to use Charles 'as a figurehead for the ship of the movement for European unity (*Der historische Karl V. eignet sich nicht zur Galionsfigur für das Schiff der Europa-Bewegung*).

Such a tendency to use the past for short-term political purposes is necessarily misleading, as Pieter Geyl showed more than half a century ago in his famous study of the changing image of Napoleon and its relation to changing political circumstances in France. We should be warned. The images of Charles the crusader, Charles the cynical follower of reason of state, and Charles the good European all become caricatures if they are taken out of context. As William Coxe observed nearly two centuries ago, 'The character of Charles V has been variously represented by the Spanish, German and French historians, and highly praised or censured according to the prejudices of country, religion or party'. In similar fashion, we would do well to heed Braudel's dismissal of one-sided interpretations of the emperor, whether in terms of financial constraints or the idea of empire, and his positive suggestion – already quoted in the epigraph to this essay – that 'The history of Charles V can only be the sum of all the possible explanations of his life, his work and his time'.

Hence the value of the third approach to Charles characteristic of the twentieth century, the approach from cultural history. The series of books and articles devoted to the `imperial idea', for example, despite their differences in interpretation, all agree in taking this idea as problematic, a historical phenomenon requiring research rather than something which can safely be taken for granted.

This essay itself is an example of the cultural approach in its concentration on the many different ways in which Charles was imagined, presented and re-presented in four and a half centuries of historical writing and many other forms of representation. A survey of this kind is more than a scholarly reaction to the pervasiveness of publicity in our time, a point which was made in the opening paragraph of this essay. By showing that each successive age has created a Charles V of its own, this survey may help to make us all more aware of our natural tendencies to see our own concerns reflected in the past.

BIBLIOGRAPHICAL ESSAY

1. The contemporary image

The standard primary sources for the career of Charles V are of course also sources for his public image, it is simply a question of reading them in a different way. The classic discussion is in the second volume of K. Brandi's biography, *Kaiser Karl V: Quellen und Erörterungen* (Munich, 1941). Visual images of Charles, normally treated as no more than 'illustrations', are of course major sources for a study of the way in which he represented himself, or was represented by others in his lifetime. Some of these primary sources have been examined with particular care.

Charles's memoirs, for example, have been studied a number of times. They survive in a Portuguese version of 1620, which was printed together with a French translation in A. Morel-Fatio, *Historiographie de Charles Quint* (Paris, 1913), 182-358. A Spanish edition has been edited by M. Fernández Alvarez, Madrid, 1960. For a more sceptical view of the text, see V. De Cadenas y Vicent, *Las supuestas memorias del emperador Carlos V* (Madrid, 1989). On the emperor's political testaments, which are also a kind of memoir, K. Brandi, 'Die politische Testamente Karls V', *Nachrichten von der Gesellschaft der Wissenschaften zu Göttingen* (Göttingen, 1930), 258-93; B. Beinert, 'Die Testamente Karls V', in P. Rassow and F. Schalk (eds.) *Karl V*, (Cologne and Graz, 1960), 21-37.

The emperor's idea of empire (or the idea of empire of those closest to him) has been the object of a series of studies by P. Rassow, *Die Kaiser-Idee Karls V* (Berlin, 1932), R. Menéndez Pidal, *La idea imperial de Carlos V* (1937: rpr Buenos Aires, 1941); F. Yates, 'Charles V and the Idea of Empire', in her *Astraea* (London, 1975), 1-28; J. A. Maravall, *Carlos V y el pensamiento politico del Renacimiento* (Madrid, 1960); H. -J. König, *Monarchia Mundi und Res Publica Christiana: Die Bedeutung des mittelalterlichen Imperium Romanum für die politischen Ideenwelt Kaiser Karls V und seiner Zeit*, Hamburg 1969; E. Van Daele, 'Het keizeridee in de vlugschriften (1531-1555)' unpublished master's thesis, University of Ghent, 1979-80; and most fully by J. H. Headley, 'The Habsburg World Empire and the Revival of Ghibellinism', *Medieval and Renaissance Studies* 7 (1978), 93-127; *id*, 'Gattinara, Erasmus and the Imperial Configuration of Humanism', *Archiv für Reformationsgeschichte* 71 (1980), 64-98; and *id*, 'Rhetoric and Reality: Messianic, Humanist and Civilian Themes in the Imperial Ethos of Gattinara', in: M. Reeves (ed.) *Prophetic Rome in the High Renaissance Period* (Oxford, 1992, 241-70. For an account of the 'world monarchy' of Charles in a longer perspective, F. Bosbach, *Monarchia Universalis: Ein politischer Leitbegriff der frühen Neuzeit* (Göttingen, 1986), 38-63.

Historians of art and literature (and occasionally plain or general historians) have produced a series of studies which are essentially concerned with the making, the interpretation and the reception of the image of Charles V. W. L. Eisler's Ph. D. thesis, 'The Impact of the Emperor Charles V upon the

Visual Arts' (Penn State University, 1983), claims, perhaps too strongly, that 'the arts played an integral role' in Charles's 'attempt to maintain his authority'. F. Checa Cremades, *Carlos V y la imagen del héroe en el Renacimiento* (Madrid, 1987), offers a general survey of visual images.

On medals of the emperor, the essential monograph is M. Bernhardt, *Bildnismedaillen Karls V* (Munich, 1919); cf. G. Habich, *Die deutschen Schaumünzen des 16. Jahrhunderts* (Munich 1929). E. J. Rosenthal, *The Palace of Charles V at Granada* (Princeton NJ, 1985), considers the palace as an expression of the emperor's self-image, while R. Wohlfeil concentrates on the paintings in 'Kriegsheld oder Friedensfürst? Eine Studie zum Bildprogramm des Palastes Karls V. in der Alhambra zu Granada', in C. Roll (ed.) *Recht und Reich im Zeitalter der Reformation, Festschrift für Horst Rabe* (Frankfurt, 1996), 57-96. Antwerp book-bindings are the subject of L. Indestage, 'Das Bild Karls V. auf Flämischen Einbänden des xvi. Jahrhunderts', *Gutenberg-Jahrbuch* (1961), 309-18.

For a survey of portraits of the emperor, R. Wohlfeil, 'Kaiser Karl V. Vom "Burgundischer Ritter" zum "Ahnherrn Österreichs"', in *Bildnis und Image: Das Portrait zwischen Intention und Rezeption*, ed. A. Köstler and E. Seidl (Cologne, 1998), 163-78. The equestrian portrait of Charles by Titian has often been discussed in print, notably by B. Beinert, 'Carlo V en Mühlberg de Tiziano', *Archivo Español de Arte* vol. 19 (1946); W. Braunfels, 'Tizians augsburger Kaiserbildnisse', *Kunstgeschichtliche Studien für Hans Kauffmann* (Berlin, 1956); E. Panofsky, *Problems in Titian, Mostly Iconographic* (New York, 1969), 82-7.

Other specialized studies of art and literature include H. W. Janson, 'A Mythological Portrait of the Emperor Charles V',

Worcester Art Museum Annual 1 (1935-6), 19-30; M. Bataillon, 'Charles Quint comme Bon Pasteur selon fray Cipriano de Huerga', *Bulletin Hispanique* 50 (1948), 398-406; F. Bologna, 'Il Carlo V di Parmigianino', *Paragone* 7 (1956); Y. Hackenbroch, 'Some Portraits of Charles V', *Metropolitan Museum of Art Bulletin* (1969), 323-32; H. Horn, *Jan Cornelisz Vermeyen: Painter of Charles V and his Conquest of Tunis* (2 vols, Doornspijk, 1989); M. Tanner, *The Last Descendants of Aeneas: the Hapsburgs and the Mythic Image of the Emperor*, New Haven, 1993.

G. Polfliet's unpublished master's thesis at the University of Ghent, 'Het imago van Karel V tot 1530' (1979-80), concentrates on the Netherlands but is not confined to that region. E. Laubach, 'Wahlpropaganda im Wahlkampf um die deutsche Königswürde 1519', *Archiv für Kulturgeschichte* 53 (1971), 207-48, defends the notion of an early sixteenth-century 'propaganda campaign'. On propaganda for Charles in the Southern Netherlands, H. Soly, 'Plechtige Intochten in de steden van de Zuidelijke Nederlanden tijdens de overgang van Middeleeuwen naar Nieuwe Tijd: communicatie, propaganda, spektakel', *Tijdschrift voor Geschiedenis* 97 (1984), 341-61. The presentation of the Africa campaign, so important for the triumphalist image of the emperor, was studied by G. Voigt, following the model of Ranke's critique of sixteenth-century historians, in *Die Geschichtschreibung über den Zug Karls V gegen Tunis* (Leipzig, 1872); cf. T. C. P. Zimmermann, 'The Publication of Paolo Giovio's Histories: Charles V and the Revision of Book 34', *La Bibliofilia* 74 (1972), 49-90, specially concerned with Giovio on Tunis. Cf. Horn, *Jan Cornelisz Vermeyen*, cited above.

The contemporary image of the Schmalkaldic War is discussed in G. Voigt, *Die Geschichtschreibung über den Schmalkaldischen*

Krieg (Leipzig, 1874); O. Waldeck, 'Die Publizistik des Schmalkaldischen Krieges', *Archiv für Reformationsgeschichte* 7 (1909-10), 1-55, and 8 (1910-11), 44-133. The best study of official historians is A. Morel-Fatio, *Historiographie de Charles Quint*, supplemented (for a historian whom Morel-Fatio missed), by M. A. Coniglione, *Bernardo Gentile, umanista siciliano* (Catania, 1948).

Although Charles is not at the centre of their attention, M. Reeves, *The Influence of Prophecy in the Later Middle Ages: a Study in Joachimism* (Oxford, 1969), and M. Bataillon, *Erasme en Espagne* (Paris, 1937), make important observations on aspects of his image.

Court ceremony and Charles's reforms of it are discussed in M. De Ferdinandy, 'Die theatralische Bedeutung des Spanischen Hofzeremoniells Kaiser Karls V', *Archiv für Kulturgeschichte* 47 (1965), 306-20, and C. Hofmann, *Das Spanische Hofzeremoniell* (Frankfurt, 1985). On the presentation of the emperor in festivals, J. Jacquot (ed.) *Fêtes et Cérémonies au temps de Charles Quint* (Paris, 1960), remains essential. The text of an early state entry is available in a modern facsimile edition with a useful introduction: S. Anglo (ed.) *La tryumphante Entree de Charles Prince des Espagnes en Bruges 1515* (Amsterdam and New York, no date but sometime in the 1970s). On his coronations, H. Heusch, 'Le sacre de Charles Quint à Aix la Chapelle', in Jacquot, 161-8; K. F. Morrison, 'History malgré lui: a neglected Bolognese account of Charles V's Coronation in Aachen', *Studia Gratiana* 15 (1972), 675-85; T. Bernardi, 'L'incoronazione di Carlo V a Bologna', *Quaderni Storici* 61 (1986), 171-200.

Charles's device, 'Plus Ultra', has been studied by M. Bataillon, 'Plus Oultre', in: Jacquot, 13-27, and by E. J. Rosenthal, 'Plus Ultra, Non Plus Ultra and the Columnar Device of the Emperor

Charles V', *Journal of the Warburg and Courtauld Institutes*, 34 (1971), and *id.*, 'The Invention of the Columnar Device of the Emperor Charles V at the court of Burgundy in Flanders in 1516', *ibid.*, 36 (1973), 198-230.

The self-presentation of the emperor Maximilian, an obvious precedent for the young Charles to follow, has been studied by a number of scholars, notably by H. O. Burger, 'Die Selbststilisierung des "letzten Ritters"', in his *Dasein heisst eine Rolle spielen: Studien zur deutschen Literaturgeschichte* (Munich, 1963), 15-35; J.-D. Müller, *Gedachtnus: Literatur und Hofgesellschaft um Maximilian I* (Munich, 1982); G. S. Williams, 'The Arthurian Model in Emperor Maximilian's Autobiographic Writings', *Sixteenth-Century Journal* 11 (1980), 3-22; L. Silver, *Marketing Maximilian* (Princeton NJ, 2008).

Comparisons between the self-presentation of the emperor and that of other early modern rulers may be pursued with the aid of R. W. Knecht, *Renaissance Warrior and Patron: the Reign of Francis I* (second edn Cambridge, 1994); A-M. Lecoq, *François I imaginaire: symbolique et politique à l'aube de la Renaissance française* (Paris, 1987); C. Woodhead and M. Kunt (eds.) *Süleyman the Magnificent and his Age* (London, 1995); P. Burke, *The Fabrication of Louis XIV* (New Haven CN, 1992).

Posthumous images

On Charles's funeral, J. Varela, *La muerte del rey: el ceremonial funerario de la monarquía española (1500-1885)* (Madrid, 1990), 35-39, 56-60; on his tomb, R. Mulcahy, *The Decoration of the Royal Basilica of El Escorial* (Cambridge, 1994), 189-211.

Bibliographical Essay

The standard secondary works on the emperor's career, from his death to the present, are of course primary sources for the study of his posthumous image. A general survey of the posthumous image is offered by P. Rassow, 'Das Bild Karls V. im Wandel der Jahrhunderte', in P. Rassow and F. Schalk (eds.) *Karl V* (Munich, 1960), 1-17.

Robertson's history has been made accessible again in a reprint of the 1792 edition in his *Works*, ed. R. B. Sher (12 vols., London 1996), vols. 3-6. On him, J. Renwick, 'The Reception of William Robertson's Historical Writings in Eighteenth-Century France', and R. B. Sher, '*Charles V* and the Book Trade: an Episode in Enlightenment Print Culture', both in S. J. Brown (ed.) *William Robertson and the Expansion of Empire* (Cambridge, 1997), 145-63 and 164-95.

The image of the emperor in Flemish popular culture has been studied by F. Heymans, 'Keizer Karel in de literatur', in J. Decavele (ed.) *Keizer tussen stropdragers. Karel V, 1500-1558* (Leuven, 1990), 195-206; J. Verberckmoes, 'The Emperor and the Peasant', in W. Thomas and B. De Groof (eds.) *Rebelión y Resistencia en el Mundo Hispánico del siglo xvii* (Leuven, 1992), 67-78; id, *Schertsen, schimpen en schateren: Geschiedenis van het lachen in de Zuidelijke Nederlanden, zestiende en zeventiende eeuw* (Nijmegen, 1998), 137-43.

On Spain, E. Gossart, 'Charles V dans l'ancien drame historique espagnole', in *Mémoires de l'Académie Royale de Belgique* vol. 18 (1924). Cf. H. Weinrich `Sprachanekdoten um Karl V', in *Wege der Sprachkultur* (Stuttgart, 1985), 181-92.

On Charles's image in historiography, little has been written, but see R. Wohlfeil, 'Kaiser Karl V. – Ahnherr der Europäischer Union?', in *Aussenseiter zwischen Mittelalter und Neuzeit: Festschrift für Hans-Jürgen Goertz zum 60. Geburtstag*, ed. N. Fischer and M. Kobelt-Groch (Leiden, 1997), 221-242. On the posthumous image of Charles in the arts, studies include J. R. Martin, *The Decoration for the Pompa Introitus Ferdinandi* (London and New York, 1972); F. Matsche, *Die Kunst im Dienst der Staatsidee Kaiser Karls VI.* (Berlin, 1981); id, 'Die Hofbibliothek in Wien als Denkmal Kaiserliche Kulturpolitik', in C. – P. Warncke (ed.), *Ikonographie der Bibliotheken* (Wiesbaden, 1992), 199-234; and F. Checa Cremades, 'La imagen de Carlos V en el reinado de Felipe II', in *Cuadernos de Arte* (1988), 55-80.

PETER BURKE TITLES PUBLISHED BY *EER*

Peter Burke
Myths, Memories, and The Representation of Identities

Peter Burke
Secret History and Historical Consciousness
From The Renaissance to Romanticism

Peter Burke
Identity, Culture and Communications in the Early Modern World

Peter Burke
What Is History Really About?
Reflections On Theory and Practice

www.ingramcontent.com/pod-product-compliance
Lightning Source LLC
Chambersburg PA
CBHW060956230426
43665CB00015B/2219